10/08

D0759601

INDIANA POLITICAL HEROES

Geoff Paddock

Indiana Historical Society Press
Indianapolis 2008

© 2008 Indiana Historical Society Press

Printed in the United States of America

This book is a publication of the
Indiana Historical Society Press
Eugene and Marilyn Glick Indiana History Center
450 West Ohio Street
Indianapolis, Indiana 46202-3269 USA
www.indianahistory.org
Telephone orders 1-800-447-1830
Fax orders 1-317-234-0562
Online orders @ http://shop.indianahistory.org

The paper in this publication meets the minimum requirements
of American National Standard for Information Sciences—Permanence of
Paper for Printed Library Materials,
ANSI Z39. 48–1984

Library of Congress Cataloging-in-Publication Data

Paddock, Geoffrey.
  Indiana political heroes / Geoffrey Paddock.
     p. cm.
  Includes index.
  ISBN 978-0-87195-268-4 (cloth : alk. paper)
  1. Politicians–Indiana–Biography. 2. Heroes–Indiana–Biography. 3.
Indiana–Politics and government. 4. Indiana–Biography. I. Title.
  F525.P33 2008
  977.2009'9–dc22
  [B]
                                2008001938

A publication of the Eli Lilly Indiana History Book Fund

With special thanks to the individuals, their families, and friends who I interviewed for this book. This book is dedicated to them with gratefulness for their service to Indiana. To Kathleen Paddock and Carl Offerle, Stephen and Barbara Paddock, and Bridget and Stevie Paddock.

Contents

Foreword

In the fall of 2000 I began to write about individuals who had served Indiana in public life in the 1960s, 1970s, and 1980s. This is the period of time I grew up in Indiana and witnessed political and governmental leaders in both parties take stands that were not always popular with their constituents. These leaders took their positions because they believed they would improve government and provide for sound public policy. Of course, some constituents felt otherwise.

I spent a considerable amount of time identifying Hoosier political leaders who had exhibited courage and conviction in their representation of our state. I interviewed one of those leaders, former Congressman J. Edward Roush, for a proposed article in the Indiana Historical Society magazine *Traces of Indiana and Midwestern History*. In early 2002 a story on Roush was published in *Traces* that concentrated on his honesty and integrity as he represented Indiana in the U.S. House of Representatives. In addition to the article on Roush, *Traces* also published an article in the fall of 2004 on the political integrity of former Indiana lieutenant governor Richard Ristine. A third article, detailing former U.S. Senator Birch Bayh's role with two U.S. Supreme Court nominees, appeared in *Traces* in early 2007. These three individuals make up three chapters in this book. The other five subjects are former U.S. Attorney

General William Ruckelshaus, former U. S. Senator Vance
Hartke, former Gary Mayor Richard Hatcher, former U.S.
Congressman John Brademas, and former Indianapolis mayor
William Hudnut.

Based on a theme of heroic leaders of our state in the
1960s, 1970s, and 1980s, I wrote about eight individuals
who served in various positions in local, state, and national
government during that time. Each was different in personality
and temperament. Each shared, however, common goals of
tenacity and a desire to serve his city, state, and country in a
way that would honor and respect his Hoosier constituency.
I have identified eight public servants who invited scrutiny to
their reputations, and risked popularity at home, by advocating
a certain policy or advancing a position on an issue. These
gentlemen were of a previous generation and born between
1919 and 1933. Most of them served during World War II, and
were individuals who stood up and made difficult decisions
about an important issue in their time.

Each of these political leaders of the 1960s, 1970s, and
1980s displayed courage and sacrifice in taking a stand that
propelled them before the public eye. Sometimes their stand
cost them political capital back home. Sometimes their stand
led to the end of their political career. Each leader showed
courage in moving forward and standing for an idea that
improved the lives of others. Their actions also inspired the
generation that followed to enter public service.

Birch Bayh (1928–)

Former U.S. Senator Birch Bayh of Indiana served
as a liberal member of the Senate for eighteen years in a
conservative state. He served as Speaker of the Indiana House
of Representatives before being elected to the Senate in 1962
at age thirty-four. He became a national leader on the issue of
presidential succession after the assassination of President John
Kennedy in 1963. Bayh wrote four constitutional amendments,
and two of them became law. These involved the presidential
succession issue and lowering the voting age from twenty-one
to eighteen. Two other amendments, establishing the Equal
Rights Amendment and abolishing the Electoral College, did
not make it through the authorization process.

Bayh is perhaps best known for opposing two of President
Richard Nixon's nominees to become justices of the U.S.
Supreme Court. These two men, Clement Haynsworth and
G. Harold Carswell, were nominated in 1969 and 1970
respectively. By leading the fight to defeat both nominees, Bayh
risked political popularity back home and became a member
of Nixon's Enemies List. Bayh made a brief run for the 1976
Democratic presidential nomination, and was defeated for
a fourth Senate term in 1980 by Quayle. Bayh continued a
distinguished career in law for many years. He is the father of
U.S. Senator Evan Bayh.

John Brademas (1927–)

A native of Mishawaka, Indiana, Brademas was the son of

Greek immigrants. After service in the navy and after receiving a doctorate at Oxford University, he returned to Indiana to enter politics. Brademas ran unsuccessfully for Congress in 1954 and 1956, but persistence paid off. He was elected to represent the Third District in 1958, the first native-born American of Greek origin elected to Congress. He served for twenty-two years, before being defeated in 1980. For the next twenty-five years, he served as president of New York University. During his time in Congress, Brademas served under six presidents and opposed Jimmy Carter's efforts to lift an arms embargo against Turkey in 1978. Brademas worked vigorously to save South Bend's Studebaker automobile plant from closing in 1963. However, he is perhaps best known for his tireless efforts to provide federal aid to public education. The congressman had the nation's leading Catholic university, Notre Dame, in his district. Yet, he also had a close association with the Indiana State Teacher's Association. In 1965 Brademas spearheaded a compromise in the language of the bill producing the "child benefit" concept. Federal aid would not be targeted to schools themselves but for children in the schools, both public and parochial. President Johnson signed the Elementary and Secondary Education Act of 1965, which began a new era in federal aid to education. Before his defeat, Brademas attained the position of majority whip, the third highest position in the House of Representatives. Brademas and his wife Mary Ellen, live in New York City.

R. Vance Hartke (1919–2003)

Hartke was the first Democratic U.S. Senator to be elected three times in Indiana. He served as a deputy prosecuting attorney for Vanderburgh County in the 1950s and was elected mayor of Evansville in 1955 at the age of thirty-six. Hartke was elected to the U.S. Senate in 1958 and was reelected twice. He wrote three books. As a senator from Indiana, he played roles in supporting civil rights, shaping Medicare, and supporting veterans. He served as chairman of the Veterans Committee in the 1970s. Hartke is perhaps best remembered for being one of the first Democratic Senators to break with President Lyndon Johnson in opposing the Vietnam War. Hartke began questioning the war effort as early as 1965, shortly after he was reelected to a second term. By 1967 he had publicly split with Johnson. Hartke's antiwar position cost him popularity at home. He narrowly won a third term in 1970. Despite a quixotic run for the Democratic presidential nomination in 1972, his popularity had taken a tumble and former Indianapolis mayor Richard Lugar defeated him in 1976. Hartke continued to serve his state and work in his law practice until nearly his last day of life in July 2003.

Richard Hatcher (1933–)

One of thirteen children raised in poverty, Hatcher never stopped dreaming about succeeding in the world around him. He was an exceptional student at Michigan City High School, worked his way through college and law school, and then settled in nearby Gary in the early 1960s. Hatcher won a seat on the Gary City Council in 1963 and saw a corrupt and bloated city government run by his fellow Democrats. Inspired to seek reform, he bucked the political establishment to run for mayor in 1967. The long-entrenched Democratic machine saw him as a dangerous reformer. After failing to stop him in the May primary, the Lake County Democratic organization even worked to elect Republican candidate Joseph Radigan in the general election, purging some five thousand black voters from the rolls. After a Federal Bureau of Investigation investigation, a federal court ordered the voters reinstated. Hatcher's home was shot at and National Guard troops were on standby along with federal marshals to supervise balloting. Hatcher defeated Radigan 39,330 to 37,941, garnering 14 percent of the white vote.

As mayor, Hatcher worked to remove gambling, gangsters, and prostitutes from downtown Gary. He also added a significant number of minorities to the police and fire departments to reflect the city's growing minority population. He oversaw the construction of three thousand new housing units and the rehabilitation of 2,400 units in his first term as mayor. He also paved seventy miles of streets and kept the peace when Martin Luther King Jr. was assassinated. Hatcher was elected mayor five times and left office in 1988 after serving twenty years. He resides in Gary.

William Hudnut III (1932–)

Hudnut began his professional life as a Presbyterian

minister, moving to Indianapolis in 1963 at the age of thirty. He became active in the community and served as pastor of the Second Presbyterian Church on the north side of the city. In 1972 he won an upset victory over his good friend Congressman Andy Jacobs Jr. and served two years as the representative of the Eleventh Congressional District in Washington, D.C., before Jacobs beat him in a rematch in 1974. When Mayor Lugar decided not to seek a third term in 1975, Hudnut jumped into the race and won a close victory in the GOP primary and then defeated businessman Robert V. Welch in November. He won landslide reelection victories in 1979, 1983, and 1987.

Hudnut sowed the seeds planted by mayors John Barton and Lugar to change the landscape and complexion of Indianapolis, particularly its downtown. The city changed from being known as "India No Place" to being a world-class city during his sixteen years as mayor. Hudnut worked with the private sector to leverage hundreds of millions of dollars to rebuild the city and bring tens of thousands of jobs to the state's capital. After an unsuccessful run at state office, he moved to suburban Maryland where he continued a successful career in local government.

Richard Ristine (1920–)

Ristine of Crawfordville, Indiana, became lieutenant governor due to a fluke provided by the Indiana Constitution. He served as a Republican state senator from Montgomery

County before being elected lieutenant governor in 1960, the same year Democrat Matt Welsh was elected governor. Ristine received more votes for the second spot than Welsh's running mate, a first in Indiana history. During his four years in office, Ristine worked in tandem to improve Indiana's economy and educational system. In 1963 Ristine broke a tie as presiding officer in the state senate to create the sales tax and raise the individual and corporate income taxes to fund state government. Ristine was excoriated by members or his own party for this move. It cost him the governorship in 1964, and his margin of defeat left him without an opportunity to run for office in the future. Ristine was interviewed in the fall of 2004.

J. Edward Roush (1920–2004)

Roush's chapter explores his uphill battle for reelection to Congress after being gerrymandered into another district by the Indiana Supreme Court. Roush, from Huntington, kept true to his progressive beliefs and lost the 1968 race to fellow Congressman E. Ross Adair. However, he won a rematch with Adair in 1970 without compromising on his views or his integrity. Roush was an environmentalist who balanced his preservation of the land by also creating three central Indiana reservoirs that provide recreation as well as flood control. He also worked diligently to create the 911 emergency response system and served as president of Huntington College. Roush was defeated for reelection in 1976 by Dan Quayle. I interviewed Roush in 2001 and 2002.

William Ruckelshaus (1932–)

Ruckelshaus was an attorney from Indianapolis when he served in the Indiana House of Representatives in the mid-1960s. Republicans tapped him to oppose Senator Birch Bayh in 1968. Despite a vigorous campaign in a solid Republican year, Ruckelshaus lost to Bayh by about seventy thousand votes. In 1969 Ruckelshaus began service in the Nixon administration as deputy attorney general. In 1973 Nixon ordered Attorney General Elliot Richardson to fire Watergate Special Prosecutor Archibald Cox in an attempt to circumvent his upcoming indicting report on the White House activities in the bungled burglary of the Democratic National Committee in 1972. In an event that became known as the Saturday Night Massacre, Nixon fired both Richardson and then Ruckelshaus after they refused to carry out his orders to fire Cox on Saturday October 20, 1973. Both men were lauded for refusing to buckle under pressure by the president. Ruckelshaus went on to serve other Republican administrations, most notably as Ronald Reagan's director of the Environmental Protection Agency in the 1980s. He and his wife, Jill, now live in the state of Washington.

1

Birch Bayh

Birch Bayh first burst on to the national political scene in 1962 when he unseated incumbent U.S. Senator Homer Capehart in Indiana by a narrow eleven-thousand-vote margin. It was perhaps the biggest Hoosier political upset of the twentieth century, and it sent the thirty-four-year-old state legislator from Shirkieville, Indiana, to Washington, D.C.

In the Senate, Bayh established himself as a forward-thinking lawmaker from a conservative state. Barely into his second term, the young Democrat gained national recognition for opposing a popular president, who relegated Bayh to the top of his enemies list when he led opposition to two of his appointments to the U.S. Supreme Court, Clement Haynsworth and G. Harold Carswell. The experience established Bayh as a national figure, tested his courage and determination to do what he felt was right for his state and for the nation, and led him to test the water as a candidate for president.

An Indiana University Law School graduate, Birch Bayh served in the Indiana legislature from 1954 to 1962 and rose in its ranks to become Speaker of the House.

Bayh, who was born on a farm near Shirkieville, Indiana, on January 22, 1928, took the oath of office for his first Senate term in January 1963. He successfully sought a coveted seat on the Judiciary Committee and also received an assignment to the subcommittee on constitutional amendments, then an obscure branch of the Judiciary Committee. He took that position and turned it into one of prominence, as he worked to craft two constitutional amendments that became law during his tenure—a provision streamlining the process for presidential succession and lowering the voting age to eighteen. Bayh proposed two other constitutional amendments, but they failed to pass.

On the Judiciary Committee, Bayh quickly gained respect as an able and prepared debater who exhibited a strong concern for the protection of individual rights as granted by the U.S. Constitution. He was a strong proponent of the civil rights laws of the 1960s and could be relied upon by President Lyndon Johnson's administration to support nominees for the U.S. Supreme Court and federal judgeships.

Bayh worked to preserve individual rights when reviewing nominations for the judiciary. In 1969 and 1970 his beliefs on this issue came into direct conflict with a new president from a different political party. In 1968 Republican Richard Nixon narrowly defeated Democrat Hubert Humphrey nationally, but received a comfortable majority in Indiana. Bayh won reelection to another six-year term that year by seventy thousand votes, defeating a formidable opponent, William

LEFT: During his time in the U.S. Senate, Bayh served alongside such powerful Democratic Party figures as Edmund Muskie of Maine. Muskie served as the vice presidential candidate under Hubert Humphrey in the 1968 presidential election and later was U.S. Secretary of State in the Jimmy Carter administration.

ABOVE: Bayh talks with his Hoosier constituents during a visit to Indianapolis. In addition to successfully pushing for passage of two constitutional amendments during his time in the U.S. Senate, Bayh also tried, but failed, to win passage of the Equal Rights Amendment and a proposal to eliminate the Electoral College.
LEFT: Bayh relaxes at a June 1967 meeting at Indianapolis's Flanner House, an African American social services agency.

Ruckelshaus, an Indiana state representative and a future Nixon appointee to the Justice Department as attorney general.

The change in government brought new policies to Washington in January 1969, as a solid conservative took the helm of the federal government. Nixon had run a campaign emphasizing strong conservative issues, such as ending the war in Vietnam with honor and not withdrawing American troops until a settlement could be reached, restoring law and order by enforcing existing federal statutes and giving law enforcement agencies more power to do so, and appointing conservative or "strict constructionists" to the federal judiciary, particularly to the Supreme Court.

Nixon wasted little time in keeping his pledge to appoint a strong conservative to the bench. In early 1969 Chief Justice Earl Warren's departure allowed Nixon to name his first nominee to the Supreme Court. Warren had been a disappointment to conservatives. A former Republican governor of California and vice presidential running mate of Thomas Dewey in 1948, Warren turned out to be one of the most liberal chief justices of the twentieth century, weighing in on numerous cases as a supporter of a broad interpretation of the law. With Warren's exit from the Supreme Court, Nixon and many conservatives saw an opportunity to nominate a judge who would be much less likely to broadly interpret the meaning of the U.S. Constitution, especially on civil rights cases.

The president's choice of Warren Burger as chief justice met little opposition in the Senate, where Burger, a conservative jurist with solid credentials, won confirmation by a comfortable margin. Trouble brewed, however, with another selection to the Court. Associate Justice Abe Fortas, who had earlier withdrawn from consideration to become chief justice, announced his retirement, effective in May 1969. To fill Fortas's place on the bench, Nixon nominated Clement Haynsworth of South Carolina, a federal judge appointed to the bench by President Dwight Eisenhower in 1957.

Haynsworth served on the U.S. Fourth Circuit Court of Appeals in Richmond, Virginia. He had solid credentials and was a true conservative. The choice had received a supposedly thorough background check from Attorney General John Mitchell. He held Haynsworth in high regard and had nearly submitted his name for chief justice when Warren retired. Haynsworth's nomination was part of Nixon's "southern strategy." The term was used during his 1972 reelection campaign when the president chose to present the image of a strong conservative who could appeal to southern Democrats. Nixon became the first Republican since Reconstruction to sweep the South in his bid for a second term, carrying every state.

While Democrats still held a comfortable majority in the U.S. Senate, the prevailing feeling in Washington was to support the president's choice for the highest court in the land, as the Senate had earlier done with the Burger nomination.

Indeed, Haynsworth's nomination was initially met with praise from both sides of the aisle. Some moderates believed Haynsworth might be among the easier jurists to work with.

As a member of the Judiciary Committee, Bayh began the task of examining the nominee, as did other committee members. Bayh initially found no decision or statement issued by Haynsworth to be objectionable. However, it was also one of the senator's responsibilities to look deeply into a record that also included moral and ethical behavior. As the committee examined the judge's personal behavior, questions about his ability to serve came forward.

Bayh's investigation first uncovered that Haynsworth had ruled in favor of a textile company that did considerable business with another company in which the judge owned stock. When questioned about this, Haynsworth admitted to the committee that he had remained a director of the company in question. In earlier testimony, however, he indicated he had resigned from all business associations and directorships when nominated for the Fourth Circuit Court of Appeals in 1957.

In another matter, the committee found the judge purchased shares of stock in a company just after participating in a court decision in which that company was involved. Haynsworth held stock in a Greenville, South Carolina, bank and had ruled in the institution's favor in another case. Labor and civil rights groups announced opposition to the nominee because of the judge's decisions. Of particular concern was his ruling in favor of the Grace Shipping Company against a worker who had been injured on the job. Haynsworth owned stock in that company. As the hearings continued into the fall, senators began to come forward to announce either their support for or opposition to the nomination.

The vote promised to be a close one. Bayh served as one of the floor leaders for the opposition. According to Bob Blaemire, an assistant to the senator, Bayh accepted the role after several of his colleagues, most notably Phil Hart of Michigan and Edward Kennedy of Massachusetts, refused. Bayh would have to rely on many Republican colleagues for a no vote, as most southern Democratic senators stated they would vote for Haynsworth, including James Eastland, chairman of the Judiciary Committee.

Bayh's opposition to the nomination came less from the judge's conservative decisions and more from what he called a "lapse in ethical judgment." He believed Haynsworth had not been forthcoming with the committee about his business dealings and that the judge was out of touch on one of the most riveting social issues of the 1960s—civil rights.

Bayh gave Haynsworth every opportunity to make amends for the past perceptions of a conflict of interest. He recalled the judge's association with businesses in which he had ruled in the past, as Haynsworth testified before the committee. "I would ask him the question in three different ways and try to give him an opportunity to state that as a member of the highest court in the United States, he would avoid such appearances of impropriety," said Bayh. "'Would you make a different

Bayh and his then twelve-year-old son Evan make an appearance at the 1968 Indiana State Fair. Evan Bayh went on to serve two terms as Indiana's governor and in 1998 won election to the U.S. Senate, winning the seat his father had lost to Dan Quayle in 1980.

decision? Would you recuse yourself from ruling in such a way, were you to be a member of the Supreme Court?' He refused to say so. He saw nothing wrong with his actions as a federal judge, and that troubled me deeply."

While the Democrats held control of the Senate, many southern Democratic senators felt compelled to support the South Carolina judge. Republican senators proved to be the most lobbied in the effort to defeat Haynsworth. Nixon, Mitchell, and presidential adviser Bryce Harlow worked to bring fellow Republicans in line behind Haynsworth's nomination. The more Bayh's investigation uncovered on the judge, however, the less likely some key GOP senators appeared to be to support his nomination. As civil rights and labor groups lobbied hard against the nomination, the intentions of the Republican senators became known.

When the final vote was taken on November 21, 1969, Republicans William Saxbe of Ohio, Hugh Scott of Pennsylvania, Bob Packwood of Oregon, John Williams of Delaware, Robert Griffin of Michigan, and John Sherman Cooper of Kentucky proved to be pivotal votes to derail the nomination. Cooper believed that even though Haynsworth had not personally profited from his decisions in cases where he held stock in companies that appeared before his court, he had violated federal statutes and judicial canons. According to Joe Rees, special assistant to Bayh from 1968 to 1973, Griffin had been angry with Mitchell for preventing the judge from testifying for a second time before the committee. He also had voiced objection to Fortas for his blemished record on personal finances and believed Haynsworth's record should be beyond reproach as well.

When all members had recorded their votes, the Haynsworth nomination went down to defeat. Seventeen Republicans voted against the nominee. Vice President Spiro Agnew, the presiding officer, dryly acknowledged, "The yeahs are 45, the nays are 55. The nomination is rejected."

Nixon had been badly wounded. He was determined to see a conservative nominated to the Supreme Court, and he promised to submit another name to the Senate in January 1970. Privately he fumed that liberals in the body, led by Bayh, had done an injustice to him and to the country. The president and the attorney general began assembling names of those in public life they deemed a threat to their political future. Bayh became one of the top entries on the "enemies list," and he began making private telephone calls from pay phones, believing his office phone had been tapped by the Republican administration. This fear was not without justification, as it was later determined that many phones had been wiretapped on Mitchell's authorization.

Bayh's effort to defeat Haynsworth cost him support in Indiana as well. Blaemire remembered the senator being booed as he rode in the pace car of the Indianapolis 500 in 1970. Nixon was popular in the state, and going against him was not considered politically wise. In addition, the senator was seen by some as the one who smeared the reputation of a federal

judge. It was one thing to oppose the president on a piece
of legislation, but it was quite another to oppose him on the
nomination of an individual to the highest court in the land.

Nixon was determined to flex his muscle and dare the
junior senator from Indiana and others to oppose his next
nominee. While some thought the Senate action might
persuade the president to submit a more moderate name,
Nixon chose a judge similar to Haynsworth—G. Harold
Carswell of Florida—on January 19, 1970. Carswell was just
as conservative as Haynsworth and drew the same opposition
from labor and civil rights groups. According to Rees, however,
unlike Haynsworth, Carswell held no personal stocks and listed
a "declining net worth," something that appeared unusual for a
man of his age and stature.

At first Bayh had a difficult time coming up with a course
of action on the Carswell nomination. His opposition to
Haynsworth had gained him stature in the Senate but had hurt
him back home. Although it looked as if Nixon was thumbing
his nose at the Senate by submitting someone equally as
distasteful as Haynsworth, Bayh did not believe it was wise
to again oppose the president. Senate Majority Leader Mike
Mansfield also appeared leery at opposing Nixon's choice.
According to Rees, Mansfield wanted to schedule a vote on the
nominee in due course.

The Nixon administration submitted Carswell's
nomination just two months after Haynsworth's defeat. Many
senators believed it would be impossible to turn back Carswell

PAID FOR BY THE BAYH COMMITTEE / 1225 19TH ST. NW

WASHINGTON, D.C. 20036 / MILTON GILBERT, TREASURER

BIRCH BAYH FOR PRESIDENT

I'm **BAYH** Partisan

Birch **Bayh** '76

A variety of campaign material for Bayh's failed run for the Democratic Party's presidential nomination in 1976. Former Georgia governor Jimmy Carter won the nomination and went on to narrowly defeat Republican Gerald Ford in the general election.

from a place on the Court. Again, southern Democrats would probably support a conservative jurist, and there did not appear to be enough northern Republican senators to reject the nomination. Bayh was reluctant to manage another floor fight and thought it would make him look vindictive. While liberal senators were concerned about some of Carswell's decisions on the bench, it did not appear that he was as controversial as Haynsworth. The Nixon administration was more confident about its new nominee.

While he did not relish a repeat of the previous fight, revelations about Carswell's segregationist past began to trouble Bayh. According to Richard Harris in his book, *Decision*, an emotional plea from a prominent civil rights activist, Clarence Mitchell of Maryland, did much to influence the senator to oppose the nomination. As Bayh learned, Carswell had an abysmal record when it came to equality of the races.

In 1948 Carswell had made a white supremacist speech, which he later recanted. Running for the Georgia legislature, he told a meeting of the American Legion, "I believe the segregation of the races is proper and the only practical and correct way of life in our states. I have always believed so, and I shall always so act. . . . I yield to no man as a fellow candidate, or as a fellow-citizen in the firm, vigorous belief in the principles of white supremacy, and I shall always be so governed in my belief of white supremacy." Bayh recalled that Carswell was questioned about the statement and asked if he believed it. "I suppose I believed it," he replied. Some on the committee wrote the statement off to youthful indiscretion. However, Republican Senator Edward Brooke of Massachusetts pointed out that Carswell was twenty-eight at the time—old enough to understand the implications of his words.

While serving as a private attorney in Tallahassee, Florida, in 1953, Carswell drew up incorporation papers for a white-only fraternity, of which he was a charter member. Three years later, while serving as a U.S. attorney in Florida, he helped incorporate a Tallahassee golf course from a public facility built partly with federal money to a private club. The purpose of this was to avoid desegregating the facility, as the law prescribed. Bayh believed it was unlikely that a U.S. attorney familiar with federal law in this area would be oblivious to the implications of such a maneuver. Brooke and others on the Judiciary Committee viewed Carswell's action as a breach of responsibility in enforcing the guarantees of equal protection under the law.

Testimony against Carswell revealed he had obstructed civil rights cases and made attempts to impede the progress of voter registration drives aimed at the black community. In 1964 civil rights volunteers were arrested and jailed for criminal trespass when they attempted to register minority voters and were denied a habeas corpus hearing for several days by Carswell. Nine clergymen who had been arrested for unlawful assembly for trying to integrate the Tallahassee airport were denied release on habeas corpus writs by Carswell until his decision was overruled by a higher court.

To the dismay of Bayh and other Judiciary Committee members, they learned Carswell had also ruled that a drugstore owner had a constitutional right to deny service to a Hispanic mother who wanted to purchase medicine for her sick child. Finally, the judge had placed a restrictive covenant on his own home, refusing to sell it to nonwhites. When confronted about these matters during hearings before the Judiciary Committee, Carswell appeared to obfuscate what had occurred, bringing his candor into question.

Senate critics pointed out that Carswell's court decisions had frequently been reversed on appeal. "He had been reversed more than any other sitting federal judge, and I did not think he was worthy to sit on the Supreme Court," said Bayh. In addition, some leading legal scholars and attorneys questioned the judge's judicial skills. In answering that charge, Senator Roman Hruska, a Republican from Nebraska, argued: "There are a lot of mediocre people in this country, and mediocrity should be represented on the Supreme Court."

The American Bar Association refused to give the candidate its endorsement, as its membership was split about evenly for and against the nominee. In addition, a letter of support for the judge was signed by just six of his eleven colleagues on the bench. Bayh viewed all of this mounting evidence as proof he should fight the nomination. With Brooke's support, he moved for recommittal, an effort to send the nomination back to the Judiciary Committee and effectively kill it before a vote could be taken by the full Senate. Carswell supporters, led by Kansas

Republican Robert Dole, persuaded a majority of the Judiciary Committee to vote against recommittal, an action that set the stage for debate on the Senate floor.

The motion for recommittal failed by a vote of 52 to 44, and it appeared the president was going to have more luck with this nominee than he did with the previous one. However, Bayh discovered that most senators opposed Carswell; they just did not prefer to send the nomination back without a recommendation. Instead they wanted to vote on it directly. As floor leader for the opposition, Bayh sensed a very close vote on this nomination. A statement by the president galvanized the opposition. Nixon said the real issue in this debate was whether the senators wanted to "substitute their own philosophy or their own subjective judgment for that of the one person entrusted by the Constitution with the power of appointment."

Bayh saw several senators who had voted against recommittal as key for defeating Carswell's nomination, and he went after them one by one. A key holdout was Republican Margaret Chase Smith of Maine. Bayh courted her, and so did the president, who invited her to the White House. As the day of the vote neared, senators began lining up and making their intentions known. Dole informed Nixon that the vote would be close and could swing on Smith's vote and perhaps one other Republican.

On April 6, 1970, Bayh's efforts again defeated a presidential nominee to the Supreme Court. The vote was 51 to 45 against Carswell's nomination. Thirteen Republicans voted against the judge. The vote reflected a widespread feeling on both sides of the aisle that Carswell did not measure up to the stature of individuals the Senate wanted to see on the Supreme Court. Many southern senators supported the president, but privately felt insulted by his choice. Republicans such as Charles Mathias of Maryland believed that voting for Carswell would be similar to "defending a mediocre racist."

The Nixon administration let its feeling be known through statements by the president and vice president. On April 7 an angry Nixon addressed the press, stating, "I have reluctantly concluded that it is impossible to get confirmation for a judge on the Supreme Court of any man who believes in the strict construction of the Constitution, as I do, if he happens to come from the south." The president bitterly accused his opponents of prejudice and "hypocrisy" and of subjecting both Haynsworth and Carswell to "vicious assaults on their intelligence and on their honesty."

Agnew said the Senate had allowed itself to be taken in by "the worst snow job of any legislative body in history." This led Bayh, Tennessee Senator Albert Gore Sr., and twenty other senators to send a letter to the president charging him with mistaking the Senate's action and pledging they would support a conservative southerner if he met "the high legal, judicial, and ethical standards which we believe are required." Republican senators Scott and James Pearson of Kansas were furious with the administration's statements. "The Senate is anxious to support the President," Scott said. "I stand ready to help muster that support and urge the nomination of an individual with impeccable credentials."

Bayh assured the public his opposition to both Haynsworth and Carswell was based on strong convictions that neither was qualified for a position on the Supreme Court. He pointed out conservative Chief Justice Burger, Nixon's first Court nominee, easily won confirmation in early 1969. At that time, the president had vowed to nominate individuals whose credentials were "beyond challenge." Bayh noted that Nixon at the time of the Burger nomination declared he would never use his appointment power to achieve a racial, religious, or geographical balance on the court.

Bayh's role in turning back the Supreme Court nominations caused his star to rise on the national political scene, and there was talk about his running for president in 1972. The day after the Carswell vote, Eric Severeid commented on a CBS news program that the Indiana senator could be a force to be reckoned with in 1972. He referred to Bayh as a midwestern John Kennedy, encompassing intelligence, charisma, and the ability to move people and accomplish great tasks.

In late 1970 and early 1971 Bayh traveled across the country to speak before Democratic groups and introduce himself to a possible new constituency as a presidential candidate. By late 1971 it seemed almost certain Bayh would enter the 1972 presidential primaries. He established a national headquarters in Washington, D.C., and his fund-raising skills were beginning to establish an enviable campaign war chest.

Bayh's presidential campaign was about to take off when his wife, Marvella, was diagnosed with breast cancer. She underwent a modified radical mastectomy on October 8, 1971. A few days later, the senator announced that he would no longer continue his exploratory run for president. "Her complete recovery may require a lengthy period of recuperation," Bayh said of his wife. "During this time, I want to be at her side—not in Miami, Milwaukee, or Los Angeles. . . . Therefore, I am not a candidate for president."

Bayh continued to clash with the Nixon administration during the 1970s, particularly over the Vietnam War. By 1973 Bayh learned he was one of some two hundred political leaders on the president's enemies list. "I concluded there were some people in life I did not want to like me," Bayh recalled. As the Watergate scandal unfolded in 1973 and 1974, the president's popularity plummeted, and so did the fortunes of many Republicans who had been aligned with him. Less than two years after his record landslide re-election, Nixon resigned from office. In 1974 Bayh won a third term against Indianapolis mayor Richard Lugar.

With his wife's health vastly improved, the three-term senator entered the Democratic presidential primary field in late 1975. He announced his candidacy at the family farm in Shirkieville and at a speech before a joint session of the Indiana General Assembly. Bayh had served in that body for eight years and was Speaker of the House for two years. In early 1976 he filed to compete in the Iowa Democratic caucuses and primary contests in New Hampshire, Massachusetts, and New York. Victory or close finishes in these early contests would help to bolster his campaign in key primaries to be held in Illinois, Wisconsin, and Pennsylvania.

Bayh finished second in the Iowa caucus to former governor Jimmy Carter of Georgia. The Hoosier senator received good reviews from the national press, which pronounced him qualified and gifted enough to be president. However, he was not as well funded as Carter. Bayh finished third in the New Hampshire primary and fifth in the Massachusetts primary, then withdrew from the race.

In late 1978 Marvella's health worsened, as her cancer returned. She died at the age of forty-six on April 24, 1979. The couple had been together for more than twenty-seven years, and they were a beloved political team in Indiana. Eulogizing his wife, Bayh said her passing brought another star to the heavens and that her life made a difference to him and the thousands who suffer from cancer.

After his wife's death, Bayh continued his service to Indiana but lost his bid for a fourth term in 1980 to Congressman Dan Quayle. Bayh's accomplishments in the Senate and for the state of Indiana were substantial. In eighteen years in Washington he accomplished much on the national stage, while bringing jobs and infrastructure improvements to his state. After his defeat, Bayh continued to work on many causes and practiced law in Indiana and Washington, D.C.

He spoke out on various issues, particularly on the rise of the religious right in the 1980s, and he was lauded for his work to promote Title IX, equal access in athletics for boys and girls in public schools and universities. His son, Evan, served as Indiana's secretary of state and won two terms as governor before winning election to the U.S. Senate.

On October 25, 2003, a ceremony renamed the federal building in Indianapolis the Birch Bayh Federal Building and United States Courthouse. For nearly two hours on a crisp sunny day, speakers including former U.S. Representative Lee Hamilton, Governor Joe Kernan, and several federal judges recapped the long and memorable career of the man who had worked to promote human justice.

FOR FURTHER READING Bayh, Birch. *One Heartbeat Away: Presidential Disability and Succession.* Indianapolis: Bobbs-Merrill, 1968. | Bayh, Marvella, with Mary Lynn Kotz. *Marvella, a Personal Journey.* New York: Harcourt Brace Jovanovich, 1979. | Harris, Richard. *Decision.* New York: Dutton, 1971. | Small, Melvin. *The Presidency of Richard Nixon.* Lawrence: University Press of Kansas, 1999.

2

John Brademas

The Elementary and Secondary Education Act of 1965 was one of the most extensive laws ever enacted, becoming the single largest source of federal support for kindergarten through twelfth grade education in the United States as part of President Lyndon Johnson's War on Poverty. One of the principal architects of this landmark legislation was former U.S. Representative John Brademas of Indiana. As a congressman from the north-central portion of the state for more than two decades, Brademas influenced many issues in Congress and rose to the position of majority whip. He used considerable diplomatic skills in bringing together different interests to craft the "child-benefit" concept: federal aid for education would not be targeted for schools themselves, but for the children in the schools, both public and parochial. In his career in Washington, D.C., Brademas became a champion of funding and reforming primary, secondary, and post-secondary education in the United States.

Brademas was born on March 2, 1927, to a Greek immigrant father and an American mother in Mishawaka, Indiana. His father was a restaurant manager and his mother taught elementary school. Growing up, Brademas spent time at his grandparents house in Swayzee, Indiana, located about ten miles west of Marion. There, he became fascinated with his grandfather's library, which contained more than seven thousand books, and acquired a love of learning and reading.

After graduating from high school in 1945, Brademas served two years in the U.S. Navy and then attended Harvard University. After graduation, he won a Rhodes scholarship and attended Oxford University, where he received his doctorate. Brademas returned home in 1954 to seek a seat in Congress. He lost that election and the following one in 1956. Persistence paid off, however, and he was elected to represent the Third Congressional District in 1958, a midterm election that saw the Democratic Party pick up forty-nine seats in the House of Representatives. Brademas became the first native-born American of Greek origin elected to Congress, and he supported a foreign policy to protect the Greek island of Cypress from Turkish aggression and potential overthrow. He actively lobbied Secretary of State Henry Kissinger to cut off military aid to Turkey, and he opposed President Jimmy Carter's lifting of the arms embargo in 1978. "I recall my Greek born father telling me when I was a child, 'We Greeks invented democracy; some of us should practice it,'" Brademas recalled.

Shortly after his election at age thirty-one, Brademas

INDIANAPOLIS STAR

During his distinguished career, John Brademas received honorary degrees from fifty-two colleges and universities. Brademas also received the Hubert H. Humphrey Award of the American Political Science Association for outstanding public service by a political scientist.

traveled to the hometown of Speaker of the House Sam
Rayburn to request a committee assignment. He asked for
and received a seat on the Education and Labor Committee,
a position he held for twenty-two years. He was known as a
tireless worker for his congressional district. In 1964, after
the closing of the Studebaker Corporation automobile plant
in South Bend, Brademas helped the city receive an $81
million contract from the government to build military and
postal vehicles. This plant later evolved into the Humvee
and Hummer operations in Mishawaka. He also worked to
create job-training programs in his district, introduced the
federal pension protection law in 1964, and played a key role
in support of a labor-reform bill in 1959 that addressed the
alleged corruption issues of organized labor.

During two decades in Congress, Brademas either
authored or was involved in writing legislation creating the
Arts and Artifacts Indemnity Acts, the National Foundation for
the Arts and Humanities Act, the Presidential Recordings and
Materials Preservation Act, and the Federal Election Campaign
Act, which was Congress's response to the Watergate scandal.
As a member of the Education and Labor Committee, he was
chief sponsor of the Arts, Humanities and Cultural Affairs
Act; the Museum Services Act; the National Commission
on Libraries and Information Services Act; the Alcohol and
Drug Abuse Education Act; and the Older Americans Act.
"John's record as a legislator illustrates a view of government's
role that addresses the unmet need of society in general and

furthers the educational and cultural opportunities of its people in particular," noted Indiana Supreme Court Justice Frank Sullivan Jr., a former aid to the congressman in the 1970s.

Brademas served with six presidents from Dwight Eisenhower through Carter, and became the third highest ranking member of the House of Representatives in 1977, when he was chosen to be majority whip. He supported the domestic legislation of the John Kennedy and Lyndon Johnson administrations that attempted to bring more opportunities to more Americans. His greatest accomplishments as a member of Congress were his efforts to improve public education and access to it by more American children. Upon entering Congress in 1959, Brademas began working on education issues. As the second ranking member of the elementary and secondary subcommittee of the Education and Labor Committee, he worked for legislation aiding medical and dental education and vocational education. Eisenhower had committed to the National Defense Education Act of 1958, which earmarked federal money for education programs "important to our national defense." It was not until Kennedy's election in 1960, however, that Congress began to look closer at a comprehensive federal education plan. With Democrats in control of the presidency and Congress in 1965, comprehensive federal legislation was proposed.

As Brademas stated in his book *The Politics of Education*, "First we—and when I say 'we,' I include Presidents, Senators, and Representatives of both parties—made a commitment

As a young congressman, Brademas shakes hands with President John Kennedy at the White House. A former supporter of two-time Democratic presidential candidate Adlai Stevenson, former governor of Illinois, Brademas noted that Stevenson had "helped make John Kennedy possible because of the way in which he [Stevenson] articulated the nexus among values, ideas, and action in the political order."

to make education accessible to those otherwise likely to be excluded. Obviously, I think of the Elementary and Secondary Education Act of 1965, which for the first time provided substantial federal funds to grade schools and high schools, with particular attention to the teaching of disadvantaged children. The financial fulcrum of that act is Title I, which provides federal funds to school districts with a large number of low-income children."

Since the mid-1940s, proponents of federal aid for public education had failed in their efforts to pass such legislation. As Brademas stated, there were three principal obstacles: "segregation, religion, and Republicans." Many Republicans and some conservative Democrats feared that federal aid meant federal control of what was taught in schools. Some conservatives, such as Republican U.S. Senator Robert Taft of Ohio, supported federal aid to education. In 1946 Taft stated during a debate that "education is primarily a state function—but in the field of education, as in the fields of health, relief, and medical care, the federal government has a secondary obligation to see that there is a basic floor under those essential services for all adults and children in the United States." Despite Taft's sentiment, many members of Congress did not want to see the federal government provide funds to local public school districts that would have strings attached. Other members, who represented large Catholic constituencies, wanted to see funds provided for parochial schools in their districts, if federal funds were provided to public schools.

In their book *An Act of Congress*, Professors Eugene
Eidenberg of the University of Minnesota and Roy Morey
of Denison University detail the history of federal aid
to education in the United States. They point out a few
important federal aid packages were passed by Congress in
1940 and 1950. The Lanham Act of 1940 provided aid for
selected communities affected by the relocation of military
personnel. In 1950 two acts were passed by Congress. The
first one provided payments to local school districts whose tax
base was affected by government contracts and installations,
Indian reservations, and federal land holdings. The second act
authorized aid for teacher salaries and building maintenance.

Building on the success of these and other pieces of
legislation that provided aid to public schools, Brademas
became optimistic that a more sweeping bill could be approved
by Congress that would provide more help for students,
particularly from disadvantaged school districts. After the 1964
election, Democrats held overwhelming majorities in both
the House and Senate. Brademas saw an opportunity to pass
legislation that would have a great affect on how education
was funded throughout the country. He worked closely with
the Johnson administration, House Education Committee
Chairman Adam Clayton Powell of New York, Congressman
Carl Perkins of Kentucky, and the Democratic Study Group
(an organization formed in 1959 to draft legislation) to
introduce House Resolution 2362 on January 28, 1965.
Brademas took on the challenge of bringing three groups of

legislators together on this bill—those who favored federal aid to public schools only, those who supported public aid to public and parochial schools, and those who opposed giving federal aid to any schools. Brademas began efforts to meet with the divergent groups to find common ground. He also served as a link between the National Education Association and groups representing the interests of parochial schools. President Johnson delivered his education message in early 1965, and

Brademas addresses his colleagues in the U.S. House of Representatives. In a 2008 speech in Indianapolis, Brademas noted that "if a Senator or Representative is skillful, and the political forces at the time make action possible, that Senator or Congressman can, without picking up the telephone to call the White House, write the laws of the land."

identical legislation was introduced in both the House and Senate in January.

The first feedback Brademas received was from a colleague, Congressman Andy Jacobs Jr. of Indianapolis. Jacobs favored aid to public schools, but as a Catholic himself, he did not favor federal aid to Catholic schools. Richard Cardinal Cushing, archbishop of Boston, thought that Catholic schools should avoid the risk of federal control by not accepting federal aid. Monsignor Frederick Hochwalt, representing the U.S. Catholic Conference, however, endorsed the premise to provide federal aid to public and parochial schools as long as there was parity. The National Education Association and the National Council of Churches favored aid to public schools but not to parochial schools, believing that such aid violated the Constitution. The U.S. Chamber of Commerce also feared federal aid would lead to a loss of state and local control of school districts.

Brademas arranged a series of informal dinner meetings to work through the concerns of these various groups. While it appeared there were enough votes in Congress to pass a federal education bill for schools in 1965, he wanted to form consensus and overcome any divisiveness about church-and-state issues among the various interest groups. Brademas wanted to see legislation passed that provided aid to schools with a formula based on need and taking into account the role of research and development. He also sought to address the issue of separation of church and state and concerns about the roles of the federal and state governments in administering educational programs. Eidenberg and Morey pointed out that Brademas took a broad view of national needs and "felt that raising educational quality was a top priority. The aspects of the bill that involved research and development and demonstration, using private as well as public groups as resources, received his vigorous support."

Brademas emphasized the importance of solving the educational problems of all children regardless of what schools they attended. Accordingly, he was instrumental in drafting "a bill to strengthen and improve educational quality and educational opportunities in the nation's elementary and secondary schools," meaning all schools, public and parochial. His "child-benefit" concept targeted federal aid to children in both public and parochial schools and was the key point in getting broad bipartisan support for passage. He worked with Perkins and Democratic Senator Wayne Morse of Oregon, the bill's Senate sponsor, to draft language that provided aid to children in certain categories, most notably based on family income. Johnson particularly liked this approach, as it tied into the War on Poverty programs of his administration.

To ensure its success, Brademas worked to convince Democratic members of the House Education Committee to stick together as legislation was drafted. Whatever specific language came out of the subcommittee needed the support of the full committee to reach the floor of the House for debate. While some Republicans objected, Brademas and many Democrats wanted to see a bill pass out of the committee with as few amendments as possible. The hope was that similar legislation would be forthcoming from the Senate and there would be fewer opportunities for the legislation to face obstacles in passage. He was particularly instrumental in drafting language that was acceptable to committee Democrats on the meaning of Title I of the bill. Brademas worked through the concerns of many committee members, the National Education Association, and the U.S. Catholic Conference.

Perhaps the biggest challenge was an amendment offered by Congresswoman Edith Green, a Democrat from Oregon. She sought to have a judicial review section in the bill that allowed school districts to challenge the allocation formula in federal courts if they felt they were being shortchanged in the funding process. This sentiment picked up many Republican supporters, including Minority Leader Gerald Ford of Michigan. Brademas and others thought this amendment was unwise and would open the legislative process to more objectionable amendments. He also felt it would cause the coalition that had been formed to crumble. Brademas and Powell kept the amendment from being adopted.

HR 2362 was enacted into law, passing both the House and Senate, by wide margins on April 9, 1965. Title I appropriated more than $1 billion initially to approximately 94 percent of the nation's school districts in 1965. Title II was a series of grants for the purchase of library resources, instructional materials, and textbooks. Funds were distributed among the states based on elementary and secondary school enrollments. Title III provided grant money to help build school buildings, and Title IV provided money for research in both public and parochial schools. Finally, Title V was designed to help strengthen state departments of education. The legislation had been written with great flexibility in how the funds could be allocated by each state. President Johnson noted that the law would "offer new hope to tens of thousands of youngsters who need attention before they ever enroll in the first grade, and it will change school dropouts to school graduates."

Standing second from left, Brademas joins other former leaders of Congress, including (to Brademas's right) Majority Leader James Wright, Representative Thomas Foley, and (seated) Speaker Thomas "Tip" O'Neill.

The Elementary and Secondary Education Act of 1965, under funding from its Title I provision, doubled the federal spending commitment to education and created curriculum programs to help disadvantaged students, provide teacher training and instructional materials, support innovative measures in schools, improve research, and strengthen state education agencies. ESEA began as a $1 billion effort to assist poor schools, communities, and children and was authorized for a five-year period ending in 1970. It provided the most money to school districts where families earned less than $2,000 a year. Title I was reauthorized every few years in the 1970s and 1980s, with major amendments added in 1994 and 2002. Those amendments to the original act were the Improving America's School Act of 1994 and the No Child Left Behind Act of 2002. ESEA was developed primarily to assist children from low-income households and give them access to a quality public education.

Part of the funding provided under the Title I provision was earmarked for a preschool program for disadvantaged children that aimed to help prepare them for school. Launched in 1965, Head Start began as an eight-week summer preschool program and quickly expanded to a full-year program because of its success. Brademas and his colleagues envisioned a program that would help millions of young children learn basic skills, benefit from nutrition, and become prepared and ready for school as they reached the first grade. The act promoted high standards for students and fostered partnerships among families, communities, and schools. Young students that were well prepared had a better opportunity to be good students and to stay in school, improving the graduation rate.

Jack Duncan served as counsel and staff director of a subcommittee for the Education and Labor Committee in the 1960s and 1970s. He recalled that ESEA was "groundbreaking legislation at the time, and a lot of compromises had to be made to get the legislation passed. One of the areas left out was language to help children with disabilities, so they could receive an education too. John [Brademas] was able to champion that issue later and spearheaded its enactment, but it took Congress ten years to pass it."

ESEA provided categorical aid to disadvantaged children in public and parochial schools. The funds were administered by state departments of education, which helped garner support from many members of Congress who did not want to see the federal government controlling the funds. Brademas saw this as a way to get more state governments involved with making key decisions about providing a quality education, particularly for impoverished children. The formula for allocating money to school districts in each state was updated in 1974. Known as the "Brademas Formula," the definition of poverty was updated from $2,000 a year for a family of four to $3,743 a year. The original 1965 formula took into account the number of poor children in a school district and the per-pupil expenditure by the state. Brademas revised the formula in 1974 to reflect changes in population and to make sure funds to smaller states and poor rural states were commensurate with funds provided to larger industrial states. A Brademas funded initiative provided aid to local school districts to assist Spanish-speaking students in 1968.

Brademas played a major roll in seeing landmark legislation affecting primary and secondary education enacted. He continued those efforts in 1966 when Powell appointed him as chairman of a task force to propose improvements to higher education. The International Education Act, authored by Brademas, authorized grants to colleges and universities for international studies and research at both the undergraduate and graduate levels. In 1970 he sponsored a bill to provide federal aid to higher educational institutions based on the cost of educating students rather than just allocating money based on the number of students enrolled on the campus. His approach actually addressed the cost of educating each student, which changed from campus to campus, and he reasoned that it cost more to instruct a student than money received in tuition and fees. He worked with Senator Claiborne Pell of Rhode Island to create legislation known as Pell Grants to give direct aid to college students to help pay their tuition. His authorship of the International Education Act, while never fully funded, provided grants to colleges and universities to support study and research on foreign countries and cultures and other important issues in international affairs. In 1970 Brademas worked across party lines with President Richard Nixon to create the National Institute of Education. The NIE set guidelines to improve the effectiveness of teaching in higher education, to make sure the taxpayers were getting "as much as we should out of the dollars we spend on education," as Nixon noted.

As an influential member of the House Education Committee, Brademas championed another legislative initiative in 1975, authoring the Education of All Handicapped Children Act, which was created to assist local school systems in providing "free appropriate public education" to all disabled children of school age. It has been credited with serving millions of children in receiving special education and related services. The legislation funded programs to train teachers in special education and supplied more therapists, psychologists, and teaching aids to serve these children. It also provided the means to include many of these students in regular classroom settings, removed other restrictions to their education, and gave many an opportunity to pursue studies in subjects previously closed to them. Brademas also wrote legislation supporting cultural institutions by creating the National Endowments for the Arts and Humanities, as well as programs to assist libraries and museums. In 1978 the Indiana congressman worked with President Carter to enact legislation to assist middle-income students with financial aid to help pay tuition for higher education.

Brademas was a natural to be a leading voice for primary, secondary, and higher education, given his education background. His mother and sister were public school teachers.

Always an exceptional student, Brademas was encouraged at an early age to "get as much education as I could take." He earned a master's degree and a doctorate while studying as a Rhodes Scholar. His inspiration to serve as a strong voice for education in this country was founded by several principals. Among them was this country's early commitment in 1787 to cede land to the states to support the building of public schools, creation of the Morrill Act that distributed federal land to build colleges and universities in the 1800s, and the establishment of the GI Bill after World War II. Before Brademas's election to Congress, the GI Bill was the most sweeping program of federal aid to education providing millions of veterans with an opportunity to go to college. His twenty-two years in the House were marked by the passage of major education legislation from the early 1960s to the late 1970s. As he stated in his book *The Politics of Education*, "the American people have come increasingly to recognize that what happens in our schools, colleges, and universities—or does NOT happen—directly affects the strength of our economy, the security of our borders, and the quality of our national life."

Not surprisingly, Brademas believes criticism of the billions of dollars spent on federal education programs over the past forty years is unjustified. He has pointed out over the years that ESEA targeted the bulk of federal aid to the neediest schoolchildren. Money was appropriated directly to fund curricula in reading, mathematics, science, problem solving, and advancing technology. Those funds have helped increase student achievement particularly in the areas of reading and mathematics. The achievement gap between white and minority students has narrowed because of Title I funds. Scholastic Aptitude Test scores have also increased due to the targeting dollars of this education act. "Compensatory education measures launched under the banner of the Great Society have demonstrated positive results," Brademas noted.

The congressman also took great pride in the results of the Head Start program. This enormously successful preschool program has boasted substantial gains for the children it has served. He wrote that "of one-third of Head Start children found to suffer from illness or a physical handicap, 75 percent had been treated; Head Start children repeatedly performed better on preschool achievement tests than poor children who had not participated in the program; and Head Start children scored higher on a 'social competence' scale which included such variables as health, self-image, motivation, curiosity, and independence."

Brademas's leadership in Congress on the issue of education was unmatched during his years representing South Bend and the Third Congressional District in Washington. "John Brademas was an intellectual in politics, and he was a man ahead of his times on the issue of education," said James Harvey, assistant staff director of a subcommittee of the Education and Labor Committee. "He was there in the 1960s saying education was a keystone for American economic life and an essential foundation in promoting democracy."

Brademas lost his seat in 1980 during a Republican landslide that ushered Ronald Reagan into office, which had an effect on federal aid to education. Had Brademas been reelected, he may well have become the first Hoosier to serve as Speaker of the House in more than a hundred years.

In early 1981 Brademas became president of New York University, the largest private university in the nation, and served in that position until 1992. He is credited with transforming the school into a premier institution for science, mathematics, and the performing arts. According to Sullivan, Brademas "raised the morale and pride of the NYU faculty,

Brademas opens the John Brademas Center for the Study of Congress's symposium on presidential and public papers. Located at New York University's Robert Wagner Graduate School of Public Service, the center, noted Brademas, seeks "to illuminate both academic and public understanding of what the Constitution designates the first branch of the federal government."

staff, and student body" and increased the university's profile in the city. In 2000 the John Brademas Center for the Study of Congress was established at the Robert Wagner School of Public Service at New York University. At the dedication ceremony, U.S. Representative Charles Rangel of New York, a member of the Center's Advisory Council, said of his former colleague: "I am delighted by the creation of the Center named in honor of my friend and former colleague John Brademas. His extraordinary commitment to examining and highlighting the essential role that Congress plays in making policy will lead to the highest caliber of work."

In 1994 President Bill Clinton appointed Brademas chairman of the President's Committee on the Arts and Humanities. Brademas is a former chairman of the board of the Federal Reserve Bank of New York and a current board member of the New York Stock Exchange and the Rockefeller Foundation. He and his wife, Doctor Mary Ellen Brademas, a dermatologist, live in New York City, where he is also chairman of the American Ditchley Foundation and a cochair of the Center for Science, Technology, and Congress. He has been awarded honorary degrees by forty-seven colleges and universities, and the U.S. Post Office in South Bend was named in his honor in 2002. In 2006 he was selected by the American Association of Museums for induction in the AAM Centennial Honor Roll as "a pioneer in the museum field" because of his cosponsorship of the legislation establishing the National Endowment of the Humanities.

While making a campaign appearance for Democratic candidates in South Bend in September of 2006, Brademas made a stark observation about the former body where he once served. He said Congress had changed for the worse since his days in the Capitol. "What is particularly striking to me is the lack of civility, of comity, of respect for different views that now characterizes the nation's capital," he said. When asked about his philosophy towards government, Brademas said he subscribed to theologian Reinhold Neibuhr's famous quotation, "Man's capacity for justice makes democracy possible; but man's inclination to injustice makes democracy necessary."

For Further Reading Brademas, John. *The Politics of Education: Conflict and Consensus on Capitol Hill.* Norman: University of Oklahoma Press, 1987. | _____. *Washington D.C. to Washington Square.* New York: Weidenfeld and Nicolson, 1986. | Eidenberg, Eugene, and Roy D. Morey. *An Act of Congress: The Legislative Process and the Making of Education Policy.* New York: Norton, 1969.

3

R. Vance Hartke

Perhaps no other conflict since the Civil War divided the country more than the Vietnam War. As the conflict escalated in the mid 1960s, Americans became disenchanted about the huge sacrifice the country was making in a land so far away. The war became the focal point of foreign policy debate, and it caused many members of Congress to first side with President Lyndon Johnson in supporting a stand for democracy in Indochina, and then to later oppose him as casualties skyrocketed and a strategy for wining seemed elusive.

One of the first members of Congress to seriously question the veracity of America's involvement in the war was U.S. Senator Vance Hartke of Indiana. A fast talking, hard hitting former prosecutor and Evansville mayor, Hartke's participation on the national stage in the discussion of how far the United States should go to protect foreign nations from the clutch of Communism when the lives of American soldiers were at stake, alienated him from his good friend and former Senate colleague Johnson.

Hartke was born in tiny Stendel, Indiana, a coal mining region in southern Pike County, on May 31, 1919. He graduated from the University of Evansville, served in the U.S. Coast Guard and the navy during World War II, and then received a law degree from Indiana University in 1948. Before his service in the war, he married Martha Tiernon in 1943, and they had seven children. The Hartke family moved to nearby Evansville after Vance completed law school, and he began a career in law and politics.

Hartke served as a deputy prosecuting attorney in Evansville and Vanderburgh County before being elected mayor in 1955. In his first year in office, he integrated the city's swimming pool, inspiring hateful telephone calls to the family home. He served only three years before running for an open seat for the U.S. Senate in a Democratic friendly year of 1958. It was said he became the first genuine retail politician in Indiana, barnstorming around the state at all hours of the day and night to meet voters at front doors, factory gates, and shopping centers. As Wayne Waymire, a former aid, later described him, his boss was a nonstop campaigner who outworked everybody. "We would pick him up in Evansville in the morning; he would make eight to ten stops before noon and spend the night in South Bend," Waymire recalled.

It proved to be a pace other successful Indiana politicians later followed. "He changed the face of Indiana politics," said

With his election to the U.S. Senate in 1958, Vance Hartke became the first Democrat from Indiana in twenty years to win election to that position.

former U.S. Representative Lee Hamilton in a 2003 interview with the *Indianapolis Star*. That election saw Hartke draw his largest electoral plurality of his career, defeating Governor Harold Handley 56 percent to 44 percent in the midterm elections. Taking his seat in the Senate in January 1959, Hartke displayed a bubbly personality and keen intellect that earned him close friendships with his colleagues, John Kennedy of Massachusetts, Johnson of Texas, Hubert Humphrey of Minnesota, and Estes Kefauver of Tennessee. Majority Leader Johnson gave Hartke choice committee assignments on the powerful Finance and Commerce committees. He and Hartke became great friends in the Senate, and Hartke strongly backed Johnson's Great Society agenda upon his succession to the presidency following Kennedy's assassination.

For eighteen years as a senator and fourteen of them as the senior senator from Indiana, Hartke was known for his tenaciousness and his ability to juggle many issues at a time. He was used to working long days and weekends for his constituents, and in his three terms Indiana bore the fruit of many Hartke initiatives, especially in promoting economic policy and federal funding for education. As a member of the Senate Finance Committee, he helped initiate the federal student-loan program. Hartke also brought federal money to Indiana for such projects as drug research, agriculture production, flood control, housing, transportation, and urban revitalization. On a national level, Hartke could be counted on as an ally to the Kennedy and Johnson administrations on such issues as civil rights, Medicare, Medicaid, the Peace Corps, clean air and water, and promoting foreign policy initiatives through negotiations. He was an active member of the Committee on Aging and in 1971 was appointed chairman of the Veteran's Affairs Committee.

Hartke's political philosophy set the tone for his service in the Senate. When asked by a high school student about his role as a senator, he replied, "A Senator must represent his constituents to the best of his ability, and be mindful of their points of view. But he can never violate his conscience and still be true to the task for which he was elected. Sometimes following conscience may put you in a lonesome minority, but if you have the courage of your convictions, there is nothing else you can do. What else can one do in good conscience but to fight for his beliefs? I believe that when you voters elected me, you expected me to vote my conscience." Hartke was often viewed as more liberal than most Hoosier voters, but he stayed in close contact with his constituents on periodic visits back home.

In the Democratic landslide of 1964, Hartke was reelected to the Senate, defeating State Senator Russell Bontrager. In his second term the seniority and clout that he had accumulated translated into greater respect for his actions. One of his new priorities in a second term was to study the Johnson policy on Southeast Asia and the growing number of troops being sent to fight a civil war between the North and South Vietnamese. It had been the United States's foreign policy for more than a decade to send advisers and then troops to help South Vietnam in its struggle to remain independent from North Vietnam. During Hartke's six years as a senator, the war had escalated under Presidents Dwight Eisenhower, Kennedy, and now Johnson. In early 1965 Hartke began to question the purpose of America's presence in this area of the world.

In fact his first pronouncements on the Vietnam situation began during his first year in the Senate. In August of 1959 Hartke had talked with General Arthur Trudeau about the

Hartke became a mainstay in the fight for civil rights in the administrations of both John Kennedy and Lyndon Johnson, including such key legislation as the Civil Rights Act and Voting Rights Act. Here, the senator appears with Coretta Scott King, the wife of civil rights activist Martin Luther King Jr.

danger of chemical weapons being used against American advisers. He also wondered how the growing presence in Vietnam might effect relations with the Soviet Union, although he was an ardent anti-Communist.

Nevertheless the senator backed the nation's foreign policy. He applauded President Kennedy for sending marines to the region in 1962 and said the American government was "trying to give them [the South Vietnamese] the means to win." An early advocate for veterans, Hartke was one of the first senators to support higher educational benefits for returning soldiers. In 1963 he boasted of his vote to provide the largest defense budget in the nation's history (more than $50 billion) that would be used to fight the biggest battles and the "smallest brush conflict in Vietnam. We have built up a fast moving arsenal of men and weapons with which to fight the jungle war of Vietnam." Yet later that year, he questioned U.S. aid being sent to the regime of South Vietnamese President Ngo Dinh Diem. Hartke said Diem was turning his presidency into a "tyrannical dictatorship" that was "nullifying the good we do through AID [U.S. Agency for International Development], the Alliance for Progress and the Peace Corps." He cosponsored a resolution with Senator Frank Church of Idaho to halt economic and military aid to Diem unless he ended martial law and repression of his people. On November 1, 1963, Diem was assassinated and his regime was overthrown. Three weeks later Kennedy was assassinated, and members of Congress lined up in support of the new Johnson administration.

By the end of 1963 there were approximately fourteen thousand troops in Vietnam, and the United States was spending $500 million to support them. General Maxwell Taylor told the senator and others that the need for American involvement would end by 1965. Hartke and many of his colleagues continued to support the policy of providing troops to calm the immediate crisis in South Vietnam and to bring about peace in the region. He supported the Gulf of Tonkin Resolution in 1964 and campaigned for re-election that year in support of the Johnson policy of containment in Southeast Asia.

In early 1965 Hartke began to question the progress being made in the war effort. In February he asked Johnson to "spell out our goals in Southeast Asia and the reasons whey we are there." While he believed in the Communist threat to the region and accepted the domino effect of countries being taken over one by one, he questioned why the United States was holding back the Communist advance with little help from its allies. He noted troops had been increased to about 21,000 and that the government was spending $2 million a day on the war effort. "The President should and must tell America, first, and the rest of the world what our posture is; what our aims are, what our interests and commitments are; how we intend to meet these commitments. We must know where we are going and what we are going to do in Vietnam," Hartke said in a speech. Still, he added: "I will support any solution that gives promise of American withdrawal if and when we can leave without simply giving the area over to the Communists. I am proud of our men in Vietnam and salute them for their dedicated efforts in maintaining a free world."

In 1966 Hartke was one of the first senators, along with Wayne Morse of Oregon and Ernest Gruening of Alaska, to question resumed bombing in North Vietnam. He wanted to work to stop the advancement of Communism, but Hartke believed the United States was shouldering too much of the burden itself and involved in an immoral bombing campaign killing innocent civilians. On January 27 Hartke and six other senators sent Johnson a letter calling for a suspension of the bombing in North Vietnam. In February he stated he would not vote to increase taxes to pay for the war, but instead work to make cuts in the foreign-aid budget to pay for the increasing cost of the American effort overseas. Hartke said he would not support unlimited escalation of the war and would not support funding at the expense of domestic programs. The senator's feelings were being noticed throughout the country and particularly by the Johnson administration.

On February 21, 1966, the *Evansville Press* reported that the Pentagon had asked veterans organizations in the state to put pressure on the senator to stop his attacks on the administration's Vietnam policy. Later that month, Hartke led a debate in the Senate requesting the president to stop the bombing campaign in North Vietnam. Senator Lee Metcalf of Montana described Hartke as a "kind of catalyst" who brought together a group of like-minded senators who had "misgivings about the war." Another senator described him as someone "not afraid to take a position. He is a person of independent judgment, energy, and drive."

On March 6, 1966, the *Washington Post* reported that Hartke was becoming a "thorn in the side" of the administration. In a nationally syndicated Rowland Evans and Robert Novak column on March 8, it was reported that Hartke was emerging as a "peace bloc leader" and was gaining influence on the issue in the Senate at the expense of being alienated from his old friend Johnson. The *Christian Science Monitor* described Hartke as a "rising political power in the Senate who had the turbidity to challenge the President on Vietnam." The *Chicago Tribune* reported on March 12 that Hartke had a right to speak out against the war and blasted Johnson Press Secretary Bill Moyers for criticizing the senator and canceling a scheduled visit between Hartke and the president. According to one news account, Johnson, who had enjoyed a very close friendship with the senator, apparently referred to him as a "two bit mayor from a two bit town." Hartke reportedly replied he did not care what the president felt about him, but Evansville was not a two-bit town.

At home, Hartke was also criticized by Hoosier banker Frank McKinney, a close friend and former chairman of the Democratic National Committee, who said "Indiana is solidly behind LBJ." He also received criticism from Indiana newspapers and fellow Democratic politicians, including Governor Roger Branigin. Speaking to the Council on World

The cover of a campaign booklet for Hartke's 1976 re-election campaign. After surviving a bruising primary fight with Congressman Philip Hayes, Hartke went down to defeat in the general election to GOP challenger Richard Lugar, the former mayor of Indianapolis.

Affairs, the senator said about the war: "We are locked into a battle that we can win and we must win. What I am trying to do along with many of my colleagues is to hasten a just and lasting solution so that more and more of our American boys will not be called upon to make that last great sacrifice in a foreign field." He went on to say that dissent on public policy should not be considered disloyal. Hartke also worried how growing expenditures for the war would effect domestic spending on poverty programs, education, clean air and water, and interstate highways, and he did not want to increase taxes to pay for the war effort because that would have an adverse effect on middle and lower income people. His son, Jan, recalled that "it hurt him to take on his close friend, Lyndon Johnson, but he was unafraid of polls or powerful Presidents. Throughout the ensuing firestorm he stood like a tower, absolutely fearless, risking it all for what he thought was right."

The growing public split between the senator and the president was apparent in May of 1966 when Hartke refused to back a Johnson appointment to the Federal Aviation Administration because of a qualifications issue. The administration then refused to appoint the senator's choices for several Department of Agriculture posts. Later that year, Hartke became more troubled as American troop size in Vietnam increased to 175,000, and a disproportionate share of the war cost and burden was being born by U.S. forces. He called for a United Nations conference to discuss how this issue could be addressed and how a political rather than a military solution could be achieved. Hartke urged consideration of a cease-fire between both sides, as he also began to publicly worry how the growing war might bring involvement from the Soviet Union and China.

Hartke became more frustrated in 1967 at the growing cost of the war—"around $56,000 a minute"—and its effect on other foreign and domestic budget items. He began to point out corruption in the South Vietnamese government and continued to rail against allies that were not supporting the effort to route out Communism in the region. He was becoming one of the Senate's leading doves along with Morse, William Fulbright, and Eugene McCarthy. In May Hartke said the government was so preoccupied with the war there appeared to be a vacuum in "leadership, national vigor, and moral strength." He stated he did not believe Johnson would run again in 1968, saying if he did the Democratic Party would be deeply divided.

Hartke and many others in the Senate saw the goal of the United States shift from building a democracy in South Vietnam and improving social and political conditions in that country to one of indiscreet bombings of North Vietnam. This was not the policy in which Johnson campaigned with Hartke in Indiana in 1964. On November 11, 1967, the senator stated that "our policy has failed in Vietnam, destroying homes and hamlets and creating a mass production of refugees. Our allies have been conspicuously absent and the American taxpayer is footing the bill. . . . Neither the Viet Cong nor North Vietnam have capitulated to our bombing escalation, and the drain on America's potential is astounding. The set back to American's goals and fulfillment is astounding." Hartke added that the United States had spent $90 billion on the war in just over two years.

In March 1968 Hartke said the war had lost its noble purpose. He criticized Johnson for not following through on a Senate Resolution to send the Vietnam issue to the Security Council of the United Nations. By now there were 500,000 troops in the region with 18,000 dead and 95,000 wounded. The escalation of the war was costing more than $50 billion a year. "I have never advocated that the U.S. should pack up and come home if there is no immediate peace agreement," Hartke said. "Assuming that no such agreement is reached in the short term future, I do advocate that the U.S. avoid a wider war, especially through penetration of international boundaries." He called for the South Vietnamese to have more responsibility for the ground war and called for a coalition government in that region.

On March 12 Senator McCarthy of Minnesota captured 42 percent of the New Hampshire Democratic primary vote, mainly as a way for voters to vent their frustration with the Johnson administration. Senator Robert Kennedy of New York entered the presidential race as an antiwar candidate on March 16, and on March 31 Johnson withdrew as a candidate for re-election. With that action, Hartke called on the president to use his "full resources to bring about negotiations and an end to the war." On July 15, he published a book titled *American Crisis in Vietnam*, and at the Democratic National Convention in August the Hoosier senator urged adoption of a platform to end the bombing of North Vietnam, work for a cease-fire under jurisdiction of the UN, support a new general election in South Vietnam with all segments participating, and begin withdrawal of American military forces within six months of the new election in South Vietnam. He also advocated establishing a Department of Peace and a Secretary of Peace in the cabinet.

In November 1968 Richard Nixon was elected president with a plan to end the war "with honor." But after nearly two years in office, the Nixon administration only escalated the war, sending troops to Laos and Cambodia and continuing the bombings in North Vietnam. In the fall of 1970 Hartke campaigned for a third term more vehemently opposed to the war than ever and facing tough criticism at home. He won re-election by less than five thousand votes against Congressman Richard Roudebush, who was handpicked by Nixon to run against him. This race was one of the closest contests in the nation and the tightest of Hartke's career in politics. First Johnson and then Nixon had tried to discourage the senator from criticizing U.S. policy on Southeast Asia, but Hartke continued to sharpen his message in the early 1970s, advocating withdrawal of military forces, opening peace talks between the two sides, promoting a cease-fire, and freeing prisoners of war. He voted in favor of legislation setting a timetable to bring the troops home, and accused Nixon of deceiving the American people with increasing troop strength and stepping up bombings.

Hartke briefly sought the Democratic presidential nomination in 1972 as an antiwar candidate. He withdrew from the race after a poor showing in the New Hampshire primary but continued to blast Nixon for his handling of the war. Over the next few years under the Nixon and Gerald Ford administrations, a cease-fire finally occurred and the war wound down as South Vietnam succumbed to the forces of the North Vietnamese. As Saigon fell in 1975, Hartke urged the Senate to play a more assertive role in the formulation of foreign policy so a president could not repeat another Vietnam. "The Vietnam War is an example of foreign policy by Presidential decree, not democratic debate," he said on May 1, 1975. Hartke advocated a stronger partnership between Congress and the executive branch in the formation of foreign affairs that he said was the vision of the founding fathers.

The senior senator from Indiana did not get to fulfill his commitment on those issues. In 1976 he sought an unprecedented fourth term, but was defeated by former Indianapolis mayor Richard Lugar. At the relatively young age of fifty-seven, Hartke began a new career as an attorney and lobbyist in Washington and in Indiana. He stayed active in state politics and encouraged many young people, including his children, to enter the field. In his later years, he formed a surprisingly close friendship with the man who defeated him,

Lugar. "If you have to get beat, you may as well get beat by the best," Hartke later said of his GOP opponent.

To Hoosiers, Hartke was a man who was not afraid to take a controversial stand. He was a strong proponent of Head Start and of Medicare in the late 1950s and early 1960s before such support was popular. "He was one of the strongest voices for Medicare. He took a real lead on that despite a lot of opposition in the state of Indiana. He was not afraid to take a tough controversial stand," recalled Hamilton in an *Indianapolis Star* interview in 2003. As chairman of the Transportation Subcommittee of the Senate Commerce Committee, Hartke worked to have automakers equip cars with seat belts and other safety equipment. He was instrumental in the creation of Amtrak and Conrail rail transportation systems in 1970, and he helped craft legislation creating student loan programs. Having served in the military during World War II and seeing the affects of the Vietnam War on young soldiers, Hartke used his chairmanship of the Veterans Affairs Committee to champion veteran's benefits and other related issues. He created the International Executive Service Corps, an organization that worked with retired businessmen, sending them to poor countries to help small businesses grow. He also won passage of a measure making kidney dialysis available to more people, leading the *Congressional Record* to cite the move as saving a half a million lives.

Hartke's early and vehement opposition to the Vietnam War may be the most lasting impression Indiana voters have of the former senator. Jan recalled how his father agonized about what action he would take regarding this issue. The senator, his wife Martha, and other children discussed the issue around the kitchen table for hours, but Hartke ultimately decided the war was morally wrong and would destroy progress on the Great Society social programs of the mid 1960s. Jan recalled how his father's action caused his friendship with the president to end, but he also recalled that Johnson reconciled with him shortly before his death in 1973, saying of Hartke "we fought with each other, but we also fought many great battles together."

Hartke recalled that his break with Johnson hurt him back home and some Democrats never forgave him for it. But he took pleasure in referring to himself as the "great dove" and one of the first political leaders of the United States to forcibly speak out against a war that divided a country for more than two decades. Hartke remained adamant to the end and content with the leadership he provided for the country into his later years. He died quietly at home on July 27, 2003, at the age of eighty-four, and was buried in Arlington National Cemetery. Lugar had seen him just two weeks before his death in the Senate dining room with a foreign diplomat. "He was vigorous, enthusiastic, and optimistic as always. I will miss Vance Hartke very much," Lugar said.

At his father's funeral, Jan eulogized him as someone who "pursued political power in the rough and tough arena of our democratic system, but he knew power was only ennobled by great achievements. He did not have much time for cynics or critics who he felt always had a too easy theory about why you should not try or help or care. Nor did he side with those who wished to denigrate the lawmaking process." Commenting on the Indiana politician's death, Secretary General of the United Nations Kofi Annan, commended Hartke's "visionary leadership and his deep commitment to peace and multilateralism."

FOR FURTHER READING Hartke, Vance. *The American Crisis in Vietnam*. Indianapolis: Bobbs-Merrill Company, 1968. | _____. *You and Your Senator*. New York: Coward-McGann, 1970. | Kaiser, Charles. *1968 in America: Music, Politics, Chaos, Counterculture, and the Shaping of a Generation*. New York: Weidenfeld and Nicolson, 1988. | LaFeber, Walter. *The Deadly Bet: LBJ, Vietnam, and the 1968 Election*. Lanham, MD: Rowman and Littlefield, 2005.

4

Richard Hatcher

On November 7, 1967, a man who was born into poverty in an area referred to as "the patch" in Michigan City, became the first African American mayor of Gary and one of the first black mayors of a major northern industrial city. Dick Hatcher made history more than forty years ago. He provided leadership for a city in transition and hope for thousands of black citizens who longed for a better life in Indiana's second largest city. To reach that pinnacle in his life, Hatcher not only fought poverty and racism, but he also had to fight a political machine that did not take to his reform-minded ways of governing.

Richard Gordon Hatcher was born in Michigan City, Indiana, on July 10, 1933. He was one of the seven surviving children of thirteen born to Carlton and Katherine Hatcher. Like millions of minorities in the 1900s, the couple had migrated to the North in search of jobs and a better way of life. Carlton worked for Pullman Standard Works of Michigan City as a molder of railroad wheels and was often laid off for parts of the year. Katherine raised a family and worked in a nearby slaughterhouse. The Hatchers had a cast-iron potbelly stove in their living room that provided the heat in the house and an icebox that was shared by another neighboring family. They often survived on powdered milk, powdered eggs, margarine, dried prunes, and potatoes.

Dick worked after school and in the summers cutting grass, trimming hedges, and scrubbing floors for wealthy families in nearby Long Beach, an affluent community on Lake Michigan just a few miles east of Michigan City. He lost his left eye when hit by a rock thrown by a friend during a daredevil stunt in 1946. His family took their meager earnings to fit him with a glass eye. His mother died of breast cancer at age fifty-three in 1947, an event that devastated her young son. Despite this tragedy, Hatcher was determined to make the best of life, as his mother would have wanted.

Graduating from high school in 1952 with excellent grades, Hatcher enrolled at Indiana University in Bloomington that fall. At IU he worked as a dishwasher and loaded lumber into railroad freight cars. He was a good student and excelled as a sprinter on the track team, but he was also interested in the civil rights issues unfolding around him. In 1953 Hatcher and others picketed Nicks Restaurant, a popular establishment on the IU campus. Black citizens were still not served by many businesses, and Nicks would not serve black customers inside the restaurant. They only allowed them to carry out food. Hatcher also participated in picketing and sit-ins at other

Upon his election as mayor of Gary, Richard Hatcher noted that the community was "a rising sun. Together, we shall beat a way; together, we shall turn darkness into light, despair into hope and promise into progress. For God's sake, for Gary's sake—let's get ourselves together."

segregated facilities, and he once quit his job as a dishwasher at Arnies Restaurant in Michigan City after a black couple was refused service. He made the dean's list at IU and after graduation decided to return to Michigan City. In 1957 he enrolled at the Valparaiso University Law School and also worked in the psychiatric ward of a hospital, administering medications and supervising mental patients.

While in law school, Hatcher got his first taste of politics, running unsuccessfully for Michigan Township Justice of the Peace in 1958. The following year he graduated from law school and moved to Gary to accept a job as a deputy prosecutor in the Lake County Prosecutor's office in Crown Point. In the following years, he began to build an alliance with prominent black leaders of Lake County and considered running for an open state legislative seat in 1962. Instead, he decided to focus on local politics and ran for the city council in 1963. Elected to an open at-large council seat, Hatcher participated in a demonstration against discrimination in housing and helped to pass a fair-housing ordinance. He worked to integrate fire and police stations and hospital wards and also led a successful fight against efforts to decrease the regulatory power of the Human Relations Commission, as proposed by Mayor Martin Katz. In addition to his service on the council, Hatcher was a member of the National Association for the Advancement of Colored People and a founder of Muigwithania, a Swahili name for a group of young black professionals with the goal of bringing different groups of people together. He and his wife, Ruthellyn

Rowles, raised a family of three children.

For his commitment to civil rights, Hatcher was deemed a radical by many white politicians in the Lake County Democratic Party. One white member of the city council even sought to have him removed from office after claiming Hatcher failed to pay several traffic violations. There was also an attempt to lure him into a drunk driving situation. This scheme failed because Hatcher does not drink, and it turned out the alleged traffic violations were fabricated. When these plots became public, it appeared to many Gary citizens that their councilman was being harassed for supporting civil rights and other government reforms.

In 1966 Hatcher was approached to run for mayor, but he initially was concerned that he had only been a resident of Gary for seven years. Nevertheless, many city leaders saw him as the best chance to elect their first black mayor in a city with a majority African American population. Hatcher had earned a reputation in his term on city council as being honest and courageous, and on January 13, 1967, he announced his candidacy, stating he would "free this community politically from the shackles of graft, corruption, inefficiency, poverty, racism, and stagnation." To become mayor, he had to first defeat Katz in the Democratic Party primary and then a strong Republican candidate in November.

As a candidate, Hatcher was seen as a fresh political breeze to some and as a threat by others. On at least three occasions, Hatcher or his campaign aides refused bribes in

the amount of $25,000, $50,000, and $100,000 to withdraw
from the race. Hatcher accused Katz of giving only token
benefits and not jobs to blacks and of being part of the corrupt
Democratic regime that had a grip on Lake County for most
of the twentieth century. He vowed to bring the corruption
to an end, fight crime, clean up slums, and bring more jobs
to unemployed minorities in the city. Hatcher also planned to
reorganize many city departments and integrate schools. On
May 2 he defeated Katz and another white Democrat in the
primary by a wide margin.

Hatcher's campaign slogan, "Let's Get Together," resonated
with many white and minority voters alike. Lake County
Democratic Chairman John Krupa said he would support
Hatcher if he denounced his former radicalism and pledged
to work with the county Democratic organization. He also
demanded that Hatcher allow the party to appoint the police
chief, fire chief, and city controller. Hatcher refused those
demands. "Too many people have worked hard in this, and
I'm not going to abdicate my responsibilities or sell them out,"
he said. When he stated he would work with the organization
but not be submerged by it, Krupa began working behind
the scenes against Hatcher and campaigning on behalf of the
Republican candidate Joseph Radigan, a furniture store owner.

The 1967 election drew national attention and eventually
national scrutiny as prominent white Democrats within the
Lake County political organization worked against Hatcher.
Led by Krupa, they continually charged the candidate as being

a radical for being associated with Doctor Martin Luther King Jr., singer Joan Baez, and actor Marlon Brando. Hatcher was called un-American for opposing continued escalation of the Vietnam War and for stating a disproportionate amount of black men were serving in the conflict. Krupa allegedly paid money to have Hatcher's yard signs torn down, and he made it very difficult for the candidate to raise money. Hatcher managed to raise $125,000 from fund-raising events with actor Harry Belefonte and civil rights leader Julian Bond, and another $60,000 at a Washington, D.C., fund-raiser attended by U.S. Senators Robert and Edward Kennedy and Vice President Hubert Humphrey, who proudly endorsed

Always popular with African American voters in Gary, Hatcher also reached out to help other black candidates. He served as chairman of Reverend Jesse Jackson's 1984 and 1988 presidential campaigns.

his candidacy. In Indiana, the state Democratic Party did
not support Hatcher. Only U.S. Senator Birch Bayh and
U.S. Representative Andrew Jacobs Jr. officially endorsed his
candidacy.

Seeing Hatcher's campaign mobilizing well in fund-
raising and organization, Krupa worked to have more than
five thousand names of African American voters purged from
the Lake County voter registration board. He also sought to
have some three thousand new names added to the rolls that
were fraudulently obtained in an effort to turn the tables on
Hatcher's campaign and give a boost to underdog Radigan.
Further, it was revealed that people were going to be paid to
vote, including prostitutes. Krupa was able to enlist the support
of many to assist in the purging of voters and the addition of
ghost names to the rolls, convincing them that Hatcher had
to be stopped because he was a radical. At least one of the
participants, Marian Tokarski, suffered a guilty conscience and
believed Hatcher was being cheated. She went to the Federal
Bureau of Investigation and brought charges against Krupa
and many of the other organizers of the plot to influence the
election.

A special three-judge panel, appointed by the federal court,
upheld that Krupa had registered fraudulent voters to the rolls
and had tried to disenfranchise thousands of black voters. The
court further warned the Lake County election board to strictly
obey and enforce election laws in their county. Governor Roger
Branigin ordered Indiana National Guard troops into the

city to be placed on alert, and federal marshals supervised the balloting.

Despite a few voting machines becoming "jammed" about midday in some heavily black precincts, election day went on with few problems. Despite Gary being heavily Democratic, Republican candidate Radigan received nearly 49 percent of the vote or 37,941. On Tuesday, November 7, 1967, Hatcher was elected mayor with 39,330 votes. Thousands of white Democratic voters crossed party lines to vote against Hatcher. One political observer of the city election stated that a majority of individuals voted "white, not Republican or Democrat." These were the white ethnic voters who had arrived in Gary to work in the steel mills for the past fifty years. They were from all parts of the world and spoke more than fifty foreign languages. In the 1964 Indiana Democratic presidential primary, they overwhelming voted for Alabama governor George Wallace instead of Indiana governor Matthew Welsh, who was a stand-in for President Lyndon Johnson that year.

Hatcher had defeated the Lake County political machine that had worked so ferociously against him, and he made history in his own right and for the civil rights movement. He prevailed by receiving more than 95 percent of the black vote and more than 10 percent of the white vote. His appeal to moderate and liberal whites came from his campaign statements to represent the entire city and to make reforms in government that would help everyone. He had spoken forcefully against graft, gambling, prostitution, and unscrupulous politicians, and the voters listened and responded.

Declaring victory, Hatcher said "our city was about to be strangled by the left hand of corruption and right hand of backwardness. You have broken that grip, and we plan to remake this city. The election showed that the Negro vote isn't for sale. We shall prove that America need not wallow in decay, that our cities can be revived, and their people rejuvenated."

According to the November 17, 1967, issue of *Time* magazine, King called Hatcher's victory, and the victory of Carl Stokes in Cleveland and Kevin White in Boston, a "one-two-three punch against backlash and bigotry." Massachusetts Senator Edward Brooke, the only African American serving in the U.S. Senate, said the victory "showed the American Negro what he can achieve through lawful means." Respected national columnist Joseph Alsop said that "Hatcher represents black power in the best American tradition."

Taking office on January 1, 1968, the thirty-four-year-old mayor stated, "Gary is a rising sun. Together we shall beat a way; together we shall turn darkness into light, despair into hope, and promise into progress. For God's sake, for Gary's sake, let's get ourselves together." In his first years as chief executive of what was then Indiana's second largest city (population 178,000), Hatcher set out on an ambitious course of reform and rejuvenation. When the largely white neighborhood of Glen Park began seriously thinking of seceding, the Hatcher administration went to work to convince

TOP: Hatcher sits alongside U.S. Senator Robert Kennedy and East Chicago mayor John Nicosia on a campaign swing through northwest Indiana on April 29, 1968, as part of Kennedy's effort to win the Indiana Democratic presidential primary. ABOVE RIGHT: Singer and dancer Sammy Davis Jr. (left) poses with Hatcher during a visit to Gary, Indiana, circa 1968.

those who lived in Glen Park that they needed to stay a part of Gary. Hatcher argued that in forming its own government and providing its own city services, taxes for Glen Park would increase by a substantial amount. He convinced residents that Gary could more efficiently provide the essential service of the neighborhood, and they decided to stay a part of the city.

One of Hatcher's first attempts to end the corrupt patronage system was to enact a merit system of employment in the city and to create a cabinet form of government that reported directly to the mayor. In his first year in office, Gary constructed some 1,600 new low- and middle-income housing units, the first since 1952. The administration cracked down on landlords, forcing them to fix up and clean up old and decaying property. The mayor worked to receive private grants to promote crime reduction, jobs for gang members, and workforce training, particularly for construction workers. Gangsters and prostitutes began to leave the downtown area after more officers, a helicopter, and thirty-three squad cars were added to the police force. As Hatcher noted in a State of the City address: "If you go to that area of any community where education is poorest, unemployment the highest, health at its worst, housing the most substandard, there too you will find crime most rampant." He also worked to see Title I funds increased to assist in the support of special education and preschool students, and he worked to get more money to build libraries and to hire teacher's aides and assistants.

According to James Lane, a professor of history at Indiana University Northwest, Hatcher had no interest "in tearing down the system. Rather he simply wanted African Americans included as full social, political, and economic powers." Hatcher sought to enhance black entrepreneurship by helping minorities gain city contracts and to bring more minority investment into the city through the Model Cities Program and revenue sharing. Hatcher called this the Gary Genesis program.

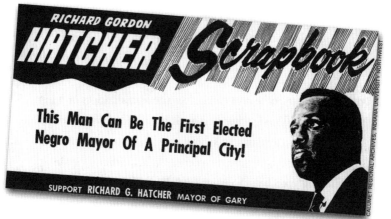

RICHARD GORDON **HATCHER** *Scrapbook*

This Man Can Be The First Elected Negro Mayor Of A Principal City!

SUPPORT **RICHARD G. HATCHER** MAYOR OF GARY

CALUMET REGIONAL ARCHIVES, INDIANA UNIVERSITY NORTHWEST

Political material distributed by Hatcher supporters during his first run for the Gary mayoral position in 1967. The Hatcher effort received support from such key national figures as Robert Kennedy, who sent Dick Tuck, an experienced political consultant, to help the campaign.

Hatcher started an enormous effort to curb air pollution
among the burgeoning steel mills. During the campaign, he
had charged that the steel mills were under assessed and that
a more adequate evaluation of the value of heavy industry
could help finance more schools. He worked to have property
reassessed to more adequately reflect the true value of business
and to bring some relief to homeowners. He was the first
mayor to see the value of his city being a convention center for
northwest Indiana, and initiated construction of a new three-
hundred room Holiday Inn downtown in 1968. The *Gary Post
Tribune*, rarely a friend to Democratic officeholders and often
critical of Hatcher during his five terms, praised the mayor
for his leadership, particularly in the areas of job creation and
expanding recreation programs. The newspaper also praised his
efforts to keep peace and calm after the assassination of King
on April 4, 1968. Hatcher personally persuaded two hundred
black students to return to school after they stormed out of
their classes and threatened violence. While other cities in
America suffered fires, looting, and rioting, Gary remained calm.

In his first years in office, Hatcher often butted heads with
city council members who accused the mayor of doing too
much traveling now that he had become a national celebrity.
Some threatened to take some of his appointment powers away
and weaken his ability to propose legislation. Hatcher remained
a strong force, however, and made his mark on the office with
his election to a second term in 1971, defeating Alexander
Williams by a wide margin in the Democratic primary and

seeing only token Republican opposition in the November election.

In 1972 Hatcher hosted a National Black Political Convention at West Side High School. The purpose was to promote his city as an attractive place for minorities to live and work, and he brought in more than four thousand delegates, including Reverend Jesse Jackson and Coretta Scott King. In his keynote address Hatcher expressed hope that Gary would "breathe the breath of life into this entire nation; for in this city are people who are eager and ready to make a new day. So my word to you this day is make a new way for Gary; make a new way for us all." The convention showcased Gary as an up-and-coming city and encouraged a new generation of black leaders to run for elective office nationwide.

In the mid-1970s Hatcher promoted an annual Founder's Day ceremony and landed the Miss Black America Pageant for a onetime event in Gary. He gained statewide fame for opposing a plan by the Northern Indiana Public Service Company to build a nuclear power plant on the lakefront in neighboring Porter County. NIPSCO, a supplier of electricity and natural gas, eventually withdrew the plan in the late 1970s. In seeking a third term in 1975, Hatcher pushed for downtown redevelopment by promoting a new civic center, hotel, marina, medical center, and minimall, and by promising improvements to the airport. Despite his efforts, federal funds were not available, and only the hotel became a reality. Despite these setbacks, Hatcher was reelected in 1975, defeating his former ally Dozier Allen in the Democratic primary.

Hatcher continued to promote his city with a "Buy in Gary" campaign to encourage more commercial businesses to be built. He worked to upgrade the bus service, completed another housing project, and ensured that transportation funds were provided to link the downtown with Interstate 65 and the Indiana Toll Road through interchanges. In 1978 he turned down an offer from President Jimmy Carter to join his senior staff in Washington, D.C., as a White House aide. Hatcher stated his decision to stay on as mayor was out of a deep commitment he felt "to the people of Gary, who have been more supportive of my efforts in this community over the past ten years. I feel we are on the threshold of major steps to rebuilding our community." Apparently, he also felt there was no clear successor as mayor, and he believed he could win a fourth term in 1979, the same year he became president of the U.S. Conference of Mayors. In fact, his previous opponent, Allen, supported him this time. U.S. Ambassador Andrew Young came in to campaign for him, and Hatcher had no trouble defeating Jesse Bell in the Democratic primary.

The following year, the Genesis Convention Center, a major component in the mayor's downtown revitalization plan, was completed at a cost of $16 million. It was paid for by the federal Community Development Block Grant program and from the Economic Development Administration with no local tax dollars involved. In 1981 a $5 million grant was secured from the federal department of Housing and Urban

Development. This money was used to convert the closed Hotel Gary into Genesis Towers, a 140-unit housing project for senior citizens and people with disabilities. This project helped spur other downtown development in the early 1980s.

For every successful project, however, there were others that never got off the ground. Despite his commitment to lead his city, Hatcher found the terrain particularly difficult at times. For example, Gary lost valuable federal dollars for a number of social programs during the administration of President Richard Nixon. Many housing projects also were halted because of a freeze in funding from HUD. Merrillville decided to incorporate and annexed a large portion of urban area so it would be out of the reach of Gary. Hatcher tried unsuccessfully to stop the move through the state legislature, predicting such a move would choke his city and prevent it from growing to the south. The U.S. Attorney's office investigated several city departments during Hatcher's third term searching for improprieties. The mayor tagged the investigations as a witchhunt by his enemies, and indeed the probe resulted in no indictments. Despite his efforts to revitalize Gary, private investment dollars were hard to come by. Suburban malls caused longtime downtown stores to close and further eroded the city's tax base. This was a growing problem in many large cities at this time. By the early 1980s, during a recessionary economy, Gary could not meet all of its financial obligations, and the city made a series of budget cuts and employee layoffs. The downtown Holiday Inn closed its doors as well. Yet, Hatcher was reelected to a fifth consecutive term in 1983, with a twenty-eight-thousand-vote landslide over City Council President Thomas Crump. Hatcher still held a considerable grasp on his city.

In the mid-1980s a series of political setbacks portended the future of the longest serving mayor of Gary. Despite reconciliation with Allen in the late 1970s, Hatcher and his onetime political ally were now feuding. He also had a political falling out with East Chicago mayor Robert Pastrick. In late 1984 Hatcher was arrested for picketing in front of the South African Embassy to protest that country's apartheid policy. He lost his position as vice chairman of the Democratic National Committee in 1985, and suffered through a six-month steel strike in 1986. This strike was a tremendous blow to the Gary economy, and it furthered the decline of the steel industry in the area. More businesses left downtown and so did people. Gary saw a steady decline in population from its high of about 185,000 in 1960 to about 150,000 by 1985. Perhaps the gravest blow occurred in spite of the mayor's efforts to bring more resources to fight crime. In 1986 Gary was labeled "America's Murder Capital" by a tabloid after a series of homicides shocked the city.

In the 1987 May primary Hatcher faced a challenge by a formidable candidate in Calumet Township Assessor Thomas Barnes, who campaigned on a "Clean Up Gary" platform and capitalized on voters' discontent with his opponent's twenty-year tenure. Barnes, like Allen and others, was an early ally of

Hatcher's, having supported his candidacy for mayor in 1967. Barnes prevented his former friend from winning a record sixth term.

Indiana State Representative Charlie Brown of Gary served as Director of the Youth Services Bureau in the Hatcher administration. He first met Hatcher as a young schoolteacher during the 1967 campaign and helped mobilize the city's educators around his election. He remembered how the mayor "was successful in getting federal money for Gary and showing the country that an African American could lead a large city. He helped spur business in his early years in office and provided honesty, integrity, and capability" during his long mayoral career. Despite being defeated, Hatcher is "still revered in Gary," said Brown. "His national connections transferred a lot of money and attention on Gary, and he became a national icon." Former U.S. Representative Jill Long Thompson first became acquainted with Hatcher when she served on the Valparaiso City Council and during her unsuccessful 1986 campaign for the U.S. Senate. "Mayor Hatcher is one of those rare public servants who instinctively knows how time, place, and policy all must come together to move a society forward," she observed. "He is also very naturally charismatic."

Hatcher reflected on his two-decade record in City Hall by stating how he had tried to provide human services to those most in need. "I've made a lot of mistakes. That's what life is about, you make mistakes, but I try to say what I believe to be the truth," he observed. "My proudest moments have been when I have seen people in this city overcome adversity in their lives and reach the point where they are self sustaining and able to support their families."

As mayor, Hatcher worked to extend civil rights to more of his constituents, provided care to children, senior citizens, and disabled people, and worked to promote minority businesses, minority entrepreneurs, and home ownership. His Office of Consumer Affairs helped prevent fraud from engulfing segments of the community. He formed the Mayor's Youth Foundation to provide athletic activities for at-risk children. Hatcher worked to find funds, sometimes through foundations or private sources, to match federal funds for downtown revitalization and neighborhood housing projects. During his time in office, Hatcher and his administration secured more than $500 million for such projects. "Gary is a city where thousands of our citizens who formerly lived in misery and despair now live in decent housing," he said in 1986. Even those who opposed the mayor saw him as a man of impeccable character, outspoken but sincere, and not a demagogue. Lane described him as a person who brought people of all races into his administration and hired the first Hispanic police officer in 1970. "My personal preference is a city made up of a multiplicity of cultural, racial, and ethnic groups," Hatcher said. "It's best when you have exposure to all kinds of people." Former U.S. Congresswoman Katie Hall, who served as Gary's deputy mayor in the mid-1970s, stated that Hatcher "didn't take us down to disgrace and shame. He lifted us. We could look up and say, yes we can. It can be done."

Hatcher instilled a pride in many Gary residents, and he accomplished much in improving services for people and in contributing to the city's economic development. In 1991 he attempted a comeback in the Democratic mayoral primary, but was defeated by Barnes. Since then, he has formed a consulting group called Richard Gordon Hatcher and Associates. He also teaches at the Valparaiso University School of Law and continues to promote the City of Gary and to fight for better working and living conditions in his community.

FOR FURTHER READING Catlin, Robert A. *Racial Politics and Urban Planning: Gary, Indiana, 1980–1989*. Lexington: University Press of Kentucky, 1993. | Lane, James B. *"City of the Century": A History of Gary, Indiana*. Bloomington: Indiana University Press, 1978. | _____. "Tie Dyes and Color Lines: Life in the Calumet Region during the 1970s." *Steel Shavings*, vol. 29, 1999. | Poinsett, Alex. *Black Power: Gary Style; The Making of Mayor Richard Gordon Hatcher*. Chicago: Johnson Publishing Company, 1970.

5

William Hudnut

In one of his published books, titled *The Hudnut Years*, Bill Hudnut talks about the transformation of Indiana's capital city from India-No-Place to India-Show-Place. Indeed, during the past thirty-five years, Indianapolis has made a transformation from large but dull midwestern town to big metropolitan city, matching the renaissance seen in Atlanta, Cleveland, and other similar sized cities. Since the early 1970s, America's twelfth largest city has become a major sports entertainment center in the country thanks to a stream of progressive mayors of both political parties. But its initial progress is primarily owed to the longest-serving mayor in the city's history, Hudnut, who performed a major coup by bringing the Baltimore Colts to Indianapolis in 1984. That accomplishment helped spur a number of downtown development projects in the 1980s.

William Herbert Hudnut III was born in Ohio on October 17, 1932. He was the third of a family lineage called to the ministry. He graduated from Princeton University in 1954

When William Hudnut first arrived in Indianapolis in 1963, he remembered being "greeted by someone who said, 'We are a town that will welcome you, and then stand back for ten years to see how you do.'"

and was ordained a Presbyterian minister in 1957 from the Union Theological Seminary in New York. Hudnut served congregations in Buffalo, New York, and Annapolis, Maryland, before coming to Indianapolis in 1963 at the age of thirty. He became the senior pastor of the Second Presbyterian Church on the far-north side of the city.

Reverend Hudnut was drawn to the ministry at an early age, but he was also drawn to public service after moving to the capital city. He was appointed to the Indianapolis Board of Public Safety by Mayor Richard Lugar in the late 1960s. In 1972 Hudnut became a candidate for a seat in the U.S. House of Representatives in the Eleventh Congressional District. In November he upset four-term incumbent Democrat Andrew Jacobs Jr. Jacobs was a popular and hardworking congressman, but was caught in the landslide re-election victory of President Richard Nixon that year, who won Indiana by a record setting seven hundred thousand votes. While in office for only two years, Hudnut sponsored seventeen bills that became law in 1973 and 1974. In the Democratic friendly year of 1974 during the Watergate scandal, Jacobs regained his seat in a rematch with Hudnut.

After his defeat Hudnut thought about returning to the pulpit, but another political opportunity crossed his path. Lugar, who lost an election to the U.S. Senate in 1974, announced he would not seek a third term as mayor of Indianapolis in 1975. This opened up an opportunity for Hudnut to seek the top city office, although he started out as an underdog in that race. After receiving the endorsement of the Marion County Republican Central Committee at a slating convention, he narrowly won the Republican nomination for mayor in the May 1975 primary by defeating John Mutz and Dan Burton. The Democratic candidate, Robert Welch, was a wealthy and respected businessman in the community. The fall race was an expensive and competitive one, with Hudnut

Hudnut (left) participates in a February 1986 groundbreaking ceremony for a new elderly housing project at the corner of Indiana Avenue and Pace Street. Joining Hudnut were: (from left) Floyd Stone, president of the local neighborhood association; Rudy Hightower, Indianapolis Housing Authority director; Bill Crawford, a state representative; Reverend Mozel Sanders; and Martha Lamkin, U.S. Housing and Urban Development area director.

winning on Election Day by about fifteen thousand votes. He was sworn into office by outgoing Mayor Lugar on January 1, 1976.

For two years, Hudnut had served as a conservative Republican representing the Eleventh Congressional District. Then he became mayor of a city of more than 750,000 people that was growing into a large metropolitan city with an expanding minority population. Hudnut knew he had to face a number of big-city problems and appeal to a new constituency. He envisioned his city growing and changing and credited his two predecessors with beginning a reawakening and forming the recently merged Indianapolis-Marion County government. Unigov, enacted under Lugar in 1970, allowed the city to grow to the Marion County borders, consolidated city and county government in most departments, and gave the new mayor a number of challenges to overcome, but also many opportunities in which to take advantage.

In his book *The Hudnut Years in Indianapolis*, Hudnut credited his two immediate predecessors—Democrat John Barton and Republican Lugar—with planting the seeds for the state's largest city to become a model of growth and redevelopment for all large communities in the country. Hudnut noted that the golden years for Indianapolis were the fifty years between 1871 and 1921 when such famous Americans as President Benjamin Harrison, Booth Tarkington, James Whitcomb Riley, Eli Lilly, Madam C. J. Walker, and T. C. Steele called this young city their home. Automotive giants Carl Fisher and James Allison brought the automobile industry to the city during those years. However, by the end of World War II, the automobile industry was comfortably settled in Detroit, and Indianapolis was seen as a grimy and dirty manufacturing town with a strong presence of the Ku Klux Klan. Racial segregation was strong and African Americans were not welcome in many parts of town. The city was deemed more conservative than most large midwestern cities, as Indianapolis leaders loathed the social and economic reforms of the New Deal and refused federal aid until the late 1960s.

Hudnut said a rebirth of the city began under the Barton administration, with the formation of the Greater Indianapolis Progress Committee. He further credited Lugar with dramatically aiding the city's rebirth with the establishment of Unigov. The Greater Indianapolis Progress Committee established a forum to discuss needs and problems and pulled together a group of concerned citizens from the private sector to advise the mayor. This committee, made up of prominent Democrats and Republicans, helped to form the beginning of a strong public-private partnership that allowed the city to successfully take on enormous projects and add jobs and income to the economy. It also brought in citizens from various community and neighborhood groups to be involved with planning for the future. The committee also formed to a government reorganization task force that recommended the consolidation that led to Unigov under Lugar.

On January 1, 1970, when consolidation occurred,

Indianapolis became the twelfth largest city in the country, jumping from a population of about 525,000 to a population of more than 750,000. In his first term as mayor, Lugar sought to streamline government and eliminate overlapping agencies in the city and the county. In his second term he became the chief executive officer of both the city and county by consolidating forty-seven previously separate boards, agencies, and commissions into a strong mayoral system with a cabinet style of management. A few large departments would operate the city's business. The mayor was elected countywide, except in the communities of Beech Grove, Lawrence, Southport, Speedway, and a few other small towns that retained their own governments. Unigov established a twenty-nine member City-County Council and also an independent corporation to run the bus company, airport, certain hospitals, libraries, and some municipal buildings and municipal and superior courts. Many elected offices were eliminated, but schools, public safety, and tax structures were not affected.

Hudnut believed a consolidated city-county government would be more efficient and a cost savings to the taxpayers. There was also a broader tax base from newly annexed suburbs. He also believed the consolidation created a wider sense of community and a spirit of civic pride. Unigov also had its critics, particularly from Democrats and minorities who felt their power had been diluted. Some residents felt it would lead to more centralized government, higher taxes, and less opportunities to participate in the process. Despite the criticism and some lawsuits filed to overturn the action, a precedent setting consolidated government had been established in the state's capital city.

The new city consolidation had distinct advantages. Hudnut set about to form an inclusive administration, welcoming input and partnerships from business, labor, neighborhoods, not-for-profit entities, and citizen activists. An imposing figure standing six feet, six inches in height, Hudnut worked his enigmatic charm and his engaging personality and wit to form coalitions of citizens. With their input, he began to work on problems to improve the quality of life in Indianapolis. He established a neighborhood advisory council to help form policies on streets, sidewalks, parks, sewers, and zoning. A neighborhood crime watch committee worked directly with law enforcement officials to detect crime. The mayor appointed more women and minorities to city positions, and he created the Tanselle/Adams Commission to deal with relations between the police department and the minority community.

The mayor worked closely with public educators to urge young people to stay drug free and to stay in school and also provided more affordable housing in the central city. Some seven thousand new units were built downtown. Financing was provided to bring more than thirty-three thousand units up to code around the city, thus upgrading many neighborhoods. During his years as mayor, Hudnut worked to provide tax incentives to bring shops and stores to blighted neighborhoods;

improved drainage, storm sewers, and other infrastructure; made facade improvements to many existing businesses; and upgraded police and fire protection throughout the city. Property taxes were raised, but a hundred thousand net new jobs were created during his tenure, and the city's tax rate was actually lower when he left office than when he arrived. The city reduced its borrowing needs, resulting in an improvement in its credit and bond ratings.

Hudnut used affirmative action to hire more minority police and firefighters and to make other improvements in public safety, particularly after the Michael Taylor incident. In September 1987 Taylor was found dead in the backseat of a police car, his hands handcuffed behind him. Many minority leaders accused the police department of brutality against Taylor, who was black. While an official investigation revealed that Taylor shot himself, many in the community never believed the official version. Hudnut worked the rest of his tenure to make inroads to the black community and smooth over relationships between minorities and the police. He worked to keep affirmative action programs throughout city government, despite opposition and even lawsuits filed by the administration of President Ronald Reagan.

Perhaps the highlight of his administration came from Hudnut's creation of the Indianapolis Project to work on improving the city's image across the country. This was a key development in moving the city towards creating the Indianapolis Sports Corporation and eventually becoming the amateur sports capital of the United States. The Indianapolis Economic Development Corporation worked with the Chamber of Commerce and other groups to create and retain jobs. Hudnut could build partnerships with Democrats and Republicans as well. He proved to be a popular leader and was easily reelected in 1979 and 1983. In 1987 he briefly sought the presidency of the University of Tennessee, but withdrew from contention after he was elected to a fourth term as mayor.

In the early 1980s as the economy started to recover from a recession, Hudnut began to dream of acquiring a professional football team to play in a new downtown stadium. Indianapolis supported a professional basketball team, the Pacers, who played at the downtown Market Square Arena and had won the American Basketball Association's championship in 1973. There was also a professional hockey team, the Racers. City officials came up with a plan to expand the Indiana Convention Center and to construct a sixty thousand-seat stadium with an inflated soft top roof built over it, primarily for professional football. Hudnut worked with business leaders, the Lilly Endowment, and Krannert Charitable Trust to match thirty million in private dollars with nearly fifty million in city funds to build the stadium. He rallied the support of the community and the Indiana General Assembly, which allowed the city to impose a 1 percent food and beverage tax to pay for part of the city's portion.

Former Republican State Representative Mitch Harper of Fort Wayne was a member of the Cities and Towns Committee

The "Keyes to the City" are presented by Hudnut to eight-year-old Beatreia Burgess during a Youth Day Service Sunday, October 23, 1983, at the Greater Saint James Missionary Baptist Church.

Hudnut plays chess with an unidentified student from Indianapolis School Number 27's chess team in May 1983.

Hudnut hands out roses during a city event. During his many years in office, Hudnut appeared at numerous ceremonies and meetings involving organizations of all kinds. He later said he hoped his epitaph will read: "He built well and he cared about people."

in the early 1980s and chairman of the House Urban Affairs Committee in the late 1980s. He was instrumental in supporting the bill that created the food and beverage tax. "This legislation had the support of Marion County Democrats like Bill Crawford and powerful Republicans like Morris Mills and Larry Borst," Harper recalled. "Creating a food and beverage tax placated the concerns of many legislators who did not want to see property taxes used to construct a stadium. This was more of a voluntary tax that Republicans, especially, could live with," he said.

Once the structure was built, the tax would cease, and no other city tax dollars or state or federal dollars would be used to support it. Tax Incremental Financing was also used to allow the city to capture some of the property taxes the stadium would generate to be used for the project. Construction began in 1982 and was completed two years later; with no assurance the city would be granted a franchise from the National Football League. Since 1978, however, Hudnut had been in contact with the owner of the Baltimore Colts. The mayor had heard the team was thinking of relocating, and he began to make overtures to attract them to Indianapolis.

With the stadium nearing completion in early 1984, the Hudnut administration began to make a serious effort to attract the Colts. In fact, Bob Irsay, the team's owner, was now actively looking for another city to relocate his operation. Hudnut and Deputy Mayor Dave Frick established a negotiating team to make an offer to move the Colts to

Indianapolis. In March 1984, Isray received from city officials a two hundred-page document detailing what Indianapolis had to offer to become home to a NFL team. In addition to the new stadium, the city would build the Colts a practice facility, guarantee the team $7 million in revenue subsidies regardless of ticket revenue, and offer them up to $12.5 million in low-interest loans to make the move. In return, the Colts would pay the city $250,000 a year to play in the new stadium,

Colts owner Bob Irsay and Hudnut raise their hands in a victory salute following the Indianapolis Colts arrival in town during a ceremony at the Hoosier Dome on April 2, 1984.

give the city 5 percent of ticket revenues, and a percentage of parking revenues, concession sales, and suite rentals. Frick and his negotiating team estimated the economic benefit to the city would be $35 million a year. The city would also benefit from substantial national name recognition. "Sports was an element in our game plan to change the image of the city back in the late 1970s, early 1980s," Frick told a reporter from the Associated Press in 2007. "It was a community effort involving the major businesses in town, combined with the not-for-profit sector and the government leadership of Indianapolis and the state itself."

The city of Baltimore could not match Indianapolis's offer, and the Colts left their home city in the early morning hours of March 29, 1984, and moved to their new home in the Hoosier Dome as it was being completed. The principal reason for leaving abruptly in the middle of night sprang from a measure passed by the Maryland State Legislature to seize all Colts property in the name of eminent domain if the franchise decided to leave Baltimore. As Maryland governor Harry Hughes prepared to sign the bill into law, Hudnut arranged literally to have Mayflower moving trucks bring Colts property to Indianapolis after a midnight departure from Baltimore. This enraged Baltimore mayor William Donald Shaefer, who accused Hudnut of stealing the team in the darkness of night. Other politicians called the action immoral. "Baltimore lost the Colts," Hudnut responded. "Indianapolis did not steal them." He also said that Shaefer was "the poorest loser I've ever met in politics."

With the Colts arrangement and the construction of the Hoosier Dome, Hudnut had taken the concept of offering economic incentives to a new level. The new stadium was not only to become home to a professional football team, but it was also attracting a number of other sporting and social events, adding to the allure of the convention center. To handle the new business from conventions and sporting events, new hotels were built. The residual effect was the beginning of a brighter and busier downtown.

The appeal of Indianapolis becoming a more sports-oriented city gained traction when a new natatorium was built on the Indiana University–Purdue University at Indianapolis campus just west of downtown. A track and field facility, tennis facility, soccer fields, and a world-class velodrome were also constructed with a combination of public and private dollars. The completion of these facilities, along with the Pan Am Plaza, helped to bring the Pan Am Games, a series of amateur sporting events that attracted athletics and fans from all over the world, to Indianapolis. Prior to the Pan Am Games, the National Sports Festival had attracted some five thousand athletes from across the country. By 1987 tens of thousands were competing in the Pan Am Games, and the city was beginning to gain the reputation of a vibrant community, offering more sports and entertainment than just the Indianapolis 500. This reputation was further cemented with the arrival of the White River State Park Games and the National Collegiate Athletic Association Final Four basketball tournament in 1991.

A study released by the Indianapolis Chamber of Commerce in 1993 stated that the economic impact of building the Hoosier Dome and attracting the subsequent sporting events added more than $1 billion to the Indianapolis economy and nearly $1.9 billion in gross revenues to businesses in the area. The study said that amateur sports had created 526 jobs related directly to the sports field and created hundreds of other jobs with the opening of shops and restaurants. The appropriation of $80 million in public and private funds to build the Hoosier Dome was considered somewhat risky at the time. The Chamber of Commerce study implied its construction had proven to be a good investment for the city. Some critics, however, charged that using sports as an economic development tool created smaller growth and lower-paying jobs than a strategy of investing efforts to attract more industry and replace the 8,700 jobs lost when Western Electric and Chrysler closed plants in the city.

Hudnut believed the city's new reputation as a center for amateur sports and home to a NFL team served as a catalyst for development in Indianapolis in the late 1980s and early 1990s, and helped to attract the kinds of jobs that would pay a good living wage. Through a series of collaborative efforts joining with other governmental entities and the private sector, Indianapolis built on the success of becoming an amateur sports center to add commerce and jobs to the local economy. Hudnut offered almost $900 million in tax

abatement to pharmaceutical giant Eli Lilly, and made a
number of infrastructure improvements, to convince it to
add to its downtown campus. A new technology center that
was developed created more than four thousand new jobs.
The mayor believed one of the most important developments
to benefit the downtown area was the location of the IUPUI
campus in the early 1960s just west of the major business
district. The university worked with the administration to
revitalize an area near the campus, located on Indiana Avenue.

One of the largest building developments in 1982 was
the partnership that resulted in the construction of the thirty-
eight story American United Life building, one block from
the Indiana Statehouse. The Hudnut administration worked
for more than eighteen months and offered tax abatement to
convince AUL to build downtown rather than move to the
suburbs from the midtown location they had outgrown. Other
buildings that added a new dimension to the downtown skyline
were the thirty-two story Market Tower, completed in 1988,
and the fifty-one story Bank One Tower, completed in 1990.
In all, thirty-four new building were constructed downtown
in the 1980s, with an investment of $2.76 billion. More than
55 percent of that total amount came from private-sector
investment. Also completed during this time was a new zoo
located just west of downtown.

The Hudnut administration also persuaded a private
developer to restore the old Union Station, built in 1888.
Added to the renovated train station, which had a city

commitment of some $17 million, was a 274-room Holiday Inn, shops, restaurants, and a food court. However, the largest downtown renovation project during the mayor's sixteen-year year term was the beginning of the Circle Centre Mall. Projects begun during the Lugar administration were completed in the late 1970s and early 1980s and helped spur more interest in the Circle Centre Mall. Those projects were the restoration of the One North Capitol building, the Hyatt Regency Hotel and Merchants Plaza complex, and the Embassy Suites Hotel. The city then borrowed $230 million, and along with state support, acquired old properties to be demolished for the new mall. While plans were scaled down from the original $750 million project, the development moved forward until the economy began to falter and commitments from retailers began to disappear. Hudnut was roundly criticized for getting the city into a speculative situation that could waste hundreds of millions of tax dollars. However, he persisted and by the late 1980s, there was enough financial support, particularly from private developers such as Melvin Simon, to begin the project. In the last months of his administration, footings for the mall were poured and the city got a commitment from Nordstrom's to build a major anchor department store.

The Circle Centre Mall was a huge investment by the city, but it paled in comparison to what the city invested to attract a major airline maintenance center for the Indianapolis International Airport. In the fall of 1991 Indianapolis was a finalist for a United Airlines maintenance facility that would service primarily its 737 jets (and later many Airbus 320 United jets) in a 2.9 million-square-foot building on some 300 acres at the airport site. It was estimated that 6,300 jobs would be created with an annual payroll of $250 million and perhaps as many as 20,000 more indirect jobs would be created in the central portion of the state, adding more than $100 million annually to the area economy. The three other cities being considered by United were Louisville, Denver, and Oklahoma City, after a number of others (including Terre Haute) were dropped from consideration earlier in the process. Hudnut and Deputy Mayor John Krauss believed Indianapolis had a good chance to be selected given the large amount of land available at the airport for such a facility. The city had made the site ready for development with infrastructure and utility improvements as well.

The mayor worked closely with Governor Evan Bayh and the state to present a competitive package for United. Their ability to cross party lines and present a partnership was much stronger than the other cities in contention. The partnership also included leaders from the private sector that Hudnut had been so successful in attracting during his administration. Officials at United noted the impressive partnership among a Democratic governor, a Republican mayor, business leaders, and labor leaders on both sides of the political aisle. "Politicians and business leaders often become adversarial, and the economy of the community suffers as a result. But that has not been true here," said Rick Street, United's vice president for airport affairs. A decision by the U.S. Postal Service to construct a new distribution center at the airport also helped. "Everything we learned about the Indianapolis airport suggested they were ready to play in the big leagues of American aviation," Street concluded.

In late October, the city-state partnership offered the most competitive package of the four remaining cities, and United selected Indianapolis. According to Hudnut, "the airport would lease the site to United. The airport [authority] would issue up to $850 million worth of tax exempt special-facility revenue bonds, which would be offset by the amount of tax increment financing bonds and other instruments United might utilize. The airport would pay back the special-facility bonds out of United's lease rentals and would pay off the tax increment financing bonds from personal property taxes on United's equipment." The state granted $15.2 million for construction costs and $159 million in tax-exempt bonds for the facility. The city issued $111.5 million in tax-exempt revenue bonds that would be secured by county option income tax funds. (Hendricks County, located just west of the airport, also participated in the arrangement with an $8 million contribution.) Hudnut was criticized for this arrangement by some who saw this as corporate welfare and an effort to buy jobs. Indeed, the public sector cost per job was estimated to be more than $100,000 for the 6,300 jobs to be created by 2004.

Hudnut, Bayh, and business and labor leaders, however, unanimously agreed this was an economic development situation in which they should participate. By investing nearly $1 billion collectively, more than 25,000 jobs could be created in central Indiana that would lead to the construction of 12,000 new homes and $100 million worth of business being done annually in the region. This was something the city and state could not pass up. As Hudnut said, "the folks in the other cities would love to have made the cut. They didn't, and we did. This is unquestionably the most significant economic development deal in the country." On November 21, 1991, the announcement of the United Airlines maintenance arrangement was made in Governor Bayh's office. Hudnut said "today is one of the greatest and most exciting days in our city's history. We are a can-do city. We are a city that says 'yes' to opportunity."

Former Fort Wayne mayor Paul Helmke viewed his colleague as a mentor when he took office in 1988. "Bill Hudnut is an example of what a mayor should be," said Helmke. "He took responsibility for becoming the head cheerleader for Indianapolis, and he had the personality and charisma to inspire people. He was an inspiration to me when I became mayor because of his great insight to what a city could be and his pragmatic problem-solving abilities."

As much as he forged large coalitions to land huge projects for the city, Hudnut also worked to obtain and retain jobs in the small-business sector. To help in that endeavor, the mayor worked to improve public infrastructure and the myriad of services a city provides to the public. As he served his last year in office in 1991, the former president of the National League of Cities offered suggestions on other areas that needed attention. He noted that a city must work with schools to see there is an educated workforce, as education is a strong part of a community's infrastructure. To attract more jobs and to improve the lives of citizens, Hudnut said a city must work to provide cleaner air and water, and work to preserve the environment. In 1991 the organization Zero Population Growth cited Indianapolis as having the best environmental health of any city its size in the nation. *City and State* magazine proclaimed Hudnut the "nation's best mayor."

Hudnut did not seek a fifth term in 1991 after having run unsuccessfully for Secretary of State against incumbent Joseph Hogsett in 1990. After leaving office, Hudnut taught at the Harvard School of Government in Boston and at the Hudson Institute in Indianapolis. In 1996 he moved to Chevy Chase, Maryland, to accept a position as Senior Resident Fellow at the Urban Land Institute (promoting quality land use), located in Washington, D.C. He entered a second career in politics by being elected to the Chevy Chase Town Board and then later as mayor of this community of some 8,600 people. Hudnut described his new hometown as a suburb of Washington that is "under tremendous stress." Chevy Chase, unlike Indianapolis, suffers from a shrinking tax base, deteriorating infrastructure, and declining resources.

During his career, Hudnut wrote four books. He is a former Phi Beta Kappa who received thirteen honorary degrees, as well as the Rosa Parks Award from the American Association of Affirmative Action and the Woodrow Wilson Award for public service from his alma mater, Princeton University. He is a member of the Citizen's Commission on Civil Rights. Hudnut acknowledged in his book *The Hudnut Years*, that the "Indianapolis story is one of qualified success. It is an ongoing saga, the final chapter will never be written. The city will change mightily in the future as it has in the past, but at the heart of the State of Indiana, there will always be . . . Indianapolis."

FOR FURTHER READING Hudnut, William, III. *The Hudnut Years in Indianapolis, 1976–1991*. Bloomington: Indiana University Press, 1995. | _____. *Indianapolis: Past, Present, and Future*. New York: Newcomen Society of the United States, 1986. | _____. *Minister/Mayor*. Philadelphia: Westminster Press, 1987.

6

Richard Ristine

During the spring of 1963, the floor of the Indiana Senate became the scene of one of the most dramatic moments in the nineteenth state's legislative history. It was there the legislature stood still for a brief moment, and a Hoosier politician—Richard Ristine—cast a deciding vote to break a tie and change the financial structure of state government. The vote would be the most significant of his public life and cast a shadow on his subsequent attempt to win election as governor.

Ristine's act of political courage came about, in part, due to a quirk in Indiana's constitution regarding voting for the top two offices in the state. In 1960 Matthew Welsh, a state senator from Vincennes, became governor by approximately twenty-three thousand votes. Welsh's Republican opponent, Lieutenant Governor Crawford Parker, had hoped to succeed outgoing GOP Governor Harold Handley. Welsh became only one of two state Democrats to win in 1960. But his running mate, Earl Utterback, a state senator from Kokomo, lost the race for lieutenant governor by approximately four thousand votes to another state senator, Ristine of Crawfordsville.

Article 5, Section 4 of the Indiana Constitution of 1851 originally provided that the names of the candidates for governor and lieutenant governor would appear on the state ballot separately and be voted on separately. This produced many interesting teams in state government when the lieutenant governor was of a different political party than that of the governor. It was not until 1974 that a constitutional amendment was ratified changing the system and providing for the names of the two offices to appear jointly upon the state ballot. Therefore, beginning in the election of 1976, a vote for governor would be considered a vote for lieutenant governor as well.

On January 9, 1961, Welsh took the oath of office as governor, and Ristine took the oath of office as lieutenant governor. Superintendent of Public Instruction William Wilson was the only other statewide Democrat to take office that day. The remaining offices of secretary of state, auditor, treasurer, and attorney general had been captured by Republicans, and those victors also took office. Republicans also won a commanding 65 to 34 majority (with one vacancy) in the house of representatives, but Democrats had a narrow 26 to 24 edge in the state senate. The Democratic margin of one seat in the state senate meant a change of one vote in either political party could have a dramatic effect on legislation.

Both Ristine and Welsh were experienced legislators who

Richard Ristine delivers a fiery acceptance speech after his nomination as the Republican candidate for lieutenant governor in 1960. During his speech, Ristine pledged to conduct an aggressive campaign all the way to election day.

had served together as state senators, and both were regarded as moderates in their respective political parties. The men liked and respected one another. Most importantly, they shared a sense of a growing problem in Indiana and the nation in the late 1950s and early 1960s—a burgeoning post–World War II population that demanded more from state government.

Welsh and Ristine had come to power campaigning on different platforms. They soon realized those platforms could merge with a genuine respect for each other's views. Both leaders realized early in the new decade that Indiana desperately needed an additional source of revenue to pave roads, build bridges, hire more public-safety officials, and, most importantly, build schools. Democratic and Republican leaders in the legislature also recognized the pending crisis. A close working relationship between the governor and the lieutenant governor would be necessary to set an agenda during the legislative sessions of 1961 and 1963. As Welsh had stated, he was fortunate Lieutenant Governor Ristine, Republican House Speaker Richard Guthrie, and Democratic House Minority Leader Birch Bayh were experienced and well-informed legislators who encouraged a cooperative approach to many of the governor's programs. Because of that approach, several measures were adopted with little controversy in 1961, including education reform, civil rights legislation, and a reorganization of several state departments.

After the 1962 midterm elections, the makeup of state government altered slightly. Bayh was now in the U.S.

Senate, and Republicans had control of both chambers of the legislature by a margin of 26 to 24 in the Senate and 56 to 44 in the House. This would make the 1963 session more difficult for Welsh, as a major tax issue would be placed before the body for debate and deliberation. The governor knew he would need to rely on bipartisanship to get his key measures through this session, including a major restructuring of the state financial system and new taxes to fund education and other programs. In early 1963, Welsh hoped he could reach a Republican legislature with his friend and now partner in state government, Ristine.

Born on January 19, 1920, Ristine was the sixth generation of his family to choose service to his community and state. His great-great-grandfather, Henry, was one of the first settlers of Crawfordsville and had served in the Indiana legislature during the 1820s; his grandfather, Theodore, sat in the state senate in the 1880s; and his father, Harley, worked as a prosecutor in Montgomery County in 1917 and 1918. Ristine graduated from Wabash College, where he had served as president of the Young Republican Club, with a bachelor's degree in 1941. Before graduating from Columbia University Law School, he enlisted as a private in the army air force. Four years later, after serving in the Philippines and Japan, he was honorably discharged as a captain. While still stationed in the air corps, Ristine served a tour of duty in Texas, where he met Mary Lou Durrett of Wichita Falls. The two married in 1946, settled in Crawfordsville, and began to raise a family.

INDIANAPOLIS STAR

LEFT: *Ristine shares his elation at being slated as the GOP candidate for governor in 1964 with his running mate, lieutenant governor hopeful John Ryan, at the Republican convention at the Indiana State Fairgrounds Coliseum.* ABOVE: *Former governor Matthew Welsh and Ristine inspect a mental health bell while both men were speakers at a 1967 meeting of the Indiana State Mental Health Association at the Murat Temple in Indianapolis, Ristine served as president of the association.*

Ristine practiced law in Crawfordsville and later managed a bank and savings and loan association. A self-described small-town lawyer, he observed that the Indiana banking system was not competitive with systems from surrounding states. In 1950 a vacancy occurred in the state senate seat representing Montgomery and Putnam counties. Ristine decided to enter politics and led the Republican ticket in Montgomery County, winning the seat and establishing himself as a young senator at age thirty. He was reelected to office in 1954 and 1958. In the state senate, he earned a reputation as a fiscal conservative but a moderate on many social issues.

As lieutenant governor, Ristine's principal interest involved creating and retaining Hoosier jobs. He was the first in that office to see a wider role to be played by the Department of Commerce in attracting industry. During his tenure, the department also worked to create new interest in Indiana as a center for tourism. In addition, Ristine spent much of his time performing the lieutenant governor's primary function— presiding over the senate. The presiding role came to the forefront during the 1963 legislative session, which changed the way Indiana taxed and governed its people for decades to come.

When Welsh and Ristine took office in 1961, the state's finances were in poor shape. The proposed two-year budget submitted by outgoing Governor Handley anticipated a deficit of more than $18.2 million. Although a state surplus of approximately $40 million was in place, using it, Welsh reasoned, would jeopardize the state's cash balance if revenue projections fell short during the biennium that ended June 30, 1963. The situation threatened a reduction of state support for public schools and universities, which would in turn force school systems to seek higher local property taxes and universities to increase tuition costs to survive the financial crisis.

To meet the demands of the budget dilemma, some in state government urged the administration to recommend a cut in state services, a reduction in salaries for some state officials, and a layoff of many state employees. Welsh noted the State's main resource for funding education, the gross income tax, was not keeping up with the financial demand as more children entered school systems each year. In fact, state aid from the income tax, as a percentage of total school costs, began to fall in the 1950s, and the shortage was being made up with increases in local property taxes. By the early 1960s, the situation had worsened, and property taxes rose rapidly to pay for the public education of thousands of new students. Welsh floated several possible tax-increase proposals before the legislators during the 1963 regular session. His objective was to raise a minimum of $220 million in additional revenue to fund the biennial budget and produce sufficient revenue on a long-term basis. Both houses were in GOP hands in 1963, although the senate control was by just one vote due to a vacancy caused by the death of Richard Newhouse. Early in the session, several Republican senators indicated they would not support any tax increases, and Welsh knew he could get nothing through the senate without Ristine's assistance.

In December 1962 the Indiana State Tax Commission had recommended a 2 percent sales tax and a one-third increase in the gross income tax to meet the revenue shortfall. A number of other proposals began to emerge. A house Republican plan, supported by Speaker Guthrie, called for enactment of a sales tax at between 2 and 3 percent. Democrats favored a graduated income tax because they thought it was fairer to Hoosier families. Still others favored imposing an income tax increase on businesses and corporations rather than on individuals. The debate came to a standstill as the legislature ran out the clock. On March 11, 1963, after sixty-one session days for the legislators, no final plan had emerged. The general assembly adjourned without addressing the financial issue, and the governor immediately called a special session.

On March 12 Ristine banged his gavel to open a joint session of the legislature. After a plea from Welsh, the lawmakers continued wrangling about the tax issue for several more days. Time for the special session was limited, as lawmakers had to complete work on the fortieth day of the special session. Nearing the deadline, legislators outlined a compromise tax program. On April 17 a conference committee presented the "2-2-2 Plan," which introduced a 2 percent retail sales tax with no exemptions, a 2 percent net income tax on individuals, and a 2 percent net income tax on corporations. The proposed revenue program had something for each political party. Still, many members in both parties told the governor they did not want to be associated with any revenue enhancements.

Welsh addresses a freedom rally in Indianapolis sponsored by the National Association for the Advancement of Colored People on August 10, 1963.

As the compromise emerged, Welsh worked with Ristine to help sell the plan to reluctant Republicans. Both Ristine and Guthrie pledge to support the plan if Welsh would deliver hesitant Democrats, particularly in the senate. Otto Bonahoom, a former state representative, remembers the tension of the debate. He saw Ristine's willingness to help shepherd the compromise plan through the legislature as showing strong leadership; Ristine came forward and seemed willing to jeopardize his career to move the package forward and put and end to the long and tedious sessions. Allan Bloom, a Fort Wayne attorney, served as a state senator from 1962 to 1970. As did Bonahoom, he favored a 3 percent sales tax plan and lower income taxes on businesses and individuals. Bloom described the senate as a "magical place" where people became acquainted through hard work and not after-hours socializing. He said Ristine's style in approaching Republican legislators to support the compromise plan showed a great understanding of the gravity of the issue. Bloom had a great passion for education, and he saw the tax increases as a necessary tool to provide good schools in Indiana. He said even when individual discussions with legislators became tenuous at best, the lieutenant governor kept his resolve and was a "100 percent gentleman."

Indeed, Ristine appeared to go above and beyond the call of duty in supporting the governor's tax program, sometimes to the chagrin of conservative GOP members. There was little doubt the lieutenant governor would run for governor in 1964, when Welsh would leave office. Some warned that support for a tax increase, no matter how noble the purpose, would doom Ristine's chances at the Republican convention and in the general election in November. He also faced losing support among Republican legislators if Welsh could not deliver enough Democratic votes to help pass the plan. Some legislators feared this arrangement could turn out to be a setup staged to embarrass the lieutenant governor by forcing him to support a tax increase that would not pass the general assembly, or worse yet, end in a deadlock. One of these legislators was Rex Early, an Indianapolis representative who later served as state GOP chairman. He charged that Welsh had shirked leadership during the session and had a responsibility to rein in a "bloated budget" of more than one billion dollars. A close ally of Guthrie and personally fond of Ristine, Early nevertheless believed that the two Republican leaders were carrying far too much of the burden on the proposed tax package.

Ristine stated he never felt pressured or betrayed during the 101 days of the two 1963 legislative sessions. He knew the state needed revenue to operate, and there was no other way to fund schools without new tax dollars. He had worked with the governor during the session and was well acquainted with and supportive of the compromise plan. He never had any doubt that backing the package was the right thing to do for the state, no matter what political repercussions he might face in 1964 or beyond.

On April 19, 1963, the house passed the Conference Committee 2-2-2 Plan by a vote of 52 to 42 for the sales tax measure and 53 to 41 for the companion corporate and individual income tax bill. The next day, the hundredth of the joint session, the bills reached the state senate. There was great pressure on senators from both sides of the tax issue. Educators and the teachers' union lobbied for support of the package, as did the Indiana Chamber of Commerce and the Indiana Farm Bureau. Representatives of organized labor, disliking the sales tax, joined with the Indiana Manufacturing Association in opposing the bills. As the day wore on, an unofficial count for passage showed only twenty-two senators lined up in support of the measure.

Late in the evening of April 20, as the time to call the vote neared on the sales tax bill, Democratic senator Walter Baran of Lake County collapsed and was carried out of the chamber. While there is evidence Baran had been in failing health and was under tremendous pressure, another rumor spread that this was an action taken to force Ristine to break a tie and politically disable him for the 1964 election. At a few minutes before midnight, the vote was taken on the tax package. Bob Peterson of Fulton County was a young Democratic senator during the special session and recalled the pressure exerted on senators to vote for or against the package. He had made up his mind early in the process to vote for the tax proposals, although his party's leader, Senator Marshall Kizer of Marshall County, opposed it. "It was the most electrifying session I participated in during three terms in the senate," Peterson recalled.

From the presiding podium, Ristine looked around and saw the display of red and green votes on the tally board. Then the action stopped; the outcome was a tie, a vote of 24 to 24. Ristine studied the board for just a few seconds, but it seemed like minutes to Bonahoom. As the vote was secured for history, Ristine picked up his gavel, brought it down forcefully, and said, "To get this session over with and to get the state moving forward again, the chair votes aye." Accordingly, the sales tax passed by a vote of 25 to 24. Bloom remembered Ristine saying just after this action that he had just lost the race for governor. Bonahoom said there was no doubt many in the chamber had just seen an unlikely event—a public servant falling on his sword for the good of the people. Peterson said Ristine's vote "no doubt sunk his political career." Some senators left the general assembly bitter, in tears, and refused to speak to Ristine. In Crawfordsville, a sign that read "Home of the 2% Sales Tax" was nailed to a tree in the lieutenant governor's front lawn.

While some were severely critical of Ristine's action, many lauded his courage. Welsh wrote in his book, *View from the State House*, that the quality and the future of the state would be preserved thanks to men of Ristine's caliber. "I particularly pay tribute to Lieutenant Governor Ristine, who acted courageously even though he knew it was jeopardizing his political future," said Welsh. He cited both Ristine and Guthrie for working to mold the compromise and then convincing their colleagues to support it. "They provided valuable counsel in the final drafting that was most helpful," he noted.

Writers for the *Indianapolis News* and the Associated Press also congratulated the lieutenant governor for his action. Ristine had cast a "vote for the future," said Ed Ziegner, political reporter for the *News*. For his part, Ristine believed it was just part of a day's work. His actions were necessary to improve Indiana's fiscal picture. The new revenue enhancements would take effect on July 1, 1963, and provided the necessary dollars to fund education and other essential state services.

Ristine decided to move on in his life and begin a campaign to become governor, announcing plans to start a campaign committee in late 1963. On January 13, 1964, Ristine announced his candidacy to succeed Welsh. Although Ristine had an impressive record on which to run for governor in 1964, he had to fight for the GOP nomination and won it only after three long ballots. His running mate for the second spot that year was State Appellate Court Judge John Ryan of Indianapolis. Democrats nominated Lafayette attorney Roger Branigin for governor and State Representative Robert Rock of Anderson for lieutenant governor. Ristine does not recall that any of his GOP convention opponents directly referred to his famous tie-breaking vote during their campaign against him. Some delegates, however, did openly blame him for voting for the tax legislation. Others in the conservative wing of the party never forgave him for backing Dwight Eisenhower over Robert

Taft, U.S. senator from Ohio, at the 1952 Republican National Convention.

Ristine left the summer convention and entered the fall contest enduring the status of underdog partly because of a divided state Republican Party, mostly because of national events. President John Kennedy's shocking assassination on November 22, 1963, led a wave of voters to be sympathetic with the Democratic Party in 1964. To add to this movement, the GOP nominated Senator Barry Goldwater of Arizona for president. Many Americans thought that the country was generally moving in the right direction and that Goldwater was too conservative. The senator's pronouncement that "extremism in the defense of liberty is no vice" only emphasized the perceived problem.

In addition, Ristine sought to succeed a Democratic governor, Welsh, who was leaving the state in good economic shape—a condition the lieutenant governor had helped to create. Finally, the qualifications of Branigin cannot be underestimated. While he had never held elective office, Branigin was a trial attorney and an extremely popular after-dinner speaker. He ran a vigorous campaign and received a boost from the landslide victory of President Lyndon Johnson. Finally, some Republican state legislative candidates publicly advocated a repeal of the tax package if they were elected.

During the campaign, Ristine stressed to voters his hard work on behalf of the state, including his efforts to bring new jobs to Indiana. He ran a formidable campaign and raised enough money to promote himself with television advertisements. Ristine's old friend Eisenhower even produced a commercial on his behalf. By November, most of the GOP had come together to support the state ticket. However, 1964 was going to be a Democratic year. Johnson beat Goldwater handily nationwide and by more than 250,000 votes in Indiana. Control of both houses of the state legislature went solidly into Democratic hands, and Branigin defeated Ristine by more than 260,000 votes in the race for governor.

Ristine's last duty as lieutenant governor was to preside at the opening session of the general assembly in January 1965, just days before leaving office. After becoming a private citizen again, Ristine moved back to Crawfordsville, where he became president of the Elston Bank. In 1967 he began working for L. S. Ayres and Company, a department store chain, as corporate personnel administrator and later as vice president for planning.

During the 1960s and 1970s, Ristine continued to work for the state's betterment, serving with such groups as the Employment Securities Commission, the Arts and Humanities Commission, and the Indiana Historical Society. He was approached to run for Congress but declined, saying he did not want to be that far away from his family. Instead of politics, Ristine invested more time in Indiana projects and became active in the Indiana State Mental Health Association. He also spent time fund-raising for Wabash College, where he had been a trustee since 1958. Over the years, he served as treasurer, director of development, and president of the Wabash College Alumni Association. He also branched out in the business world, serving as chairman of the Federal Home Loan Bank for Indiana and Michigan, chairman of Meridian Mutual Insurance Company, and executive vice president of the Eli Lilly Endowment Inc.

Ristine retired in 1993 and moved to Leland, Michigan, where he had enjoyed cool summers as a child. Reflecting on a long career in both the public and private sectors, Ristine had no regrets about his many decisions, particularly his most famous as lieutenant governor: "The repercussions of that vote were simply not important to me." His service to the state was cited by Governor Frank O'Bannon when he awarded Ristine his ninth Sagamore of the Wabash on January 29, 2001. Public service is a noble calling, and fighting for an issue and standing up for principle is more important than experiencing political gain, particularly in Ristine's generation. Perhaps no Hoosier has exemplified that spirit any better than Richard Ristine.

FOR FURTHER READING Walsh, Justin E. *The Centennial History of the Indiana General Assembly, 1816–1978*. Indianapolis: Select Committee on the Centennial History of the Indiana General Assembly, 1987. | _____. *A Biographical Directory of the Indiana General Assembly, Volume 2, 1900–1984*. Indianapolis: Select Committee on the Centennial History of the Indiana General Assembly, 1984. | Welsh, Matthew E. *View from the State House: Recollections and Reflections, 1961–1965*. Indianapolis: Indiana Historical Bureau, 1981.

7

J. Edward Roush

Two words that seldom appear together are "politician" and "honest." In the 1960s and 1970s, however, Indiana congressman J. Edward Roush earned the moniker Honest Ed Roush. Throughout the Fifth Congressional District in north-central Indiana, Roush was regarded as a man of his word and a public servant who established a close bond with his constituents. No bribes or scandals were ever associated with Roush, elected to Congress five times between 1958 and 1966, and he, along with most of the Hoosier State, enjoyed the optimism associated with much of this era in the nation's history. That optimism and faith in government, though, would be severely tested as the country entered the painful year of 1968.

Roush's parents were both born in Huntington County, Indiana, but moved to Oklahoma to find work in the oil fields shortly after their marriage. J. Edward Roush was born in Barnsdall, Osage County, Oklahoma, on September 12, 1920.

The family moved back to Huntington in 1924, however, when the elder Roush became ill (he died in 1933). After receiving his education in the local public schools, Roush attended Huntington College, a Christian liberal arts college owned by the Church of the United Brethren in Christ, graduating in 1942. Also that year, Roush enlisted in the army, and a year later he married his college sweetheart, Marjorie Pauline (Polly) Borton. The couple eventually had four children.

During World War II, Roush served as a combat infantry officer in the Battle of the Bulge. Germans surrounded his battalion for five days and attacked it with heavy machine-gun fire. Roush was not wounded, but he suffered severe frostbite in both feet that required a four-month hospitalization in England. He later received the Bronze Star. After the war, Roush served as an army reserve officer. In 1948 he graduated from the Indiana University School of Law and subsequently saw a political opportunity appear—a chance to run for the state legislature. Walking door to door in the fall for his campaign, Roush began a practice that he later repeated as a member of Congress. He walked for miles, from one end of the district to the other, to meet every available voter.

Roush's tenure in the legislature lasted just two years, as he was recalled to active duty during the Korean War in 1950. Stationed in Germany, he withdrew as a candidate for re-election to the Indiana General Assembly to fulfill his second tour of duty to his country. His wife, Polly, ran in his place. Despite a strong campaign to succeed her husband, she lost.

During his time in Congress, J. Edward Roush won the respect of legislators from both political parties for his integrity and hard work. In his book relating his twenty-eight-year career as House doorkeeper, William "Fishbait" Miller praised Roush as "one of the boys who didn't have to be written up."

Coming home to Indiana in 1952, Roush once again practiced law in Huntington.

In 1954 Roush decided to reenter politics, running and winning election as Huntington County prosecutor, a position he held for one four-year term. Four years later, he ran as an upstart against a well-entrenched Republican incumbent, John Beamer, for the U.S. Fifth District congressional seat. Aided by hard work, a vigorous door-to-door campaign, and the benefit of a good Democratic year nationally, Roush defeated Beamer by approximately 1,300 votes.

For his first attempt at re-election, Roush fought a tough campaign against GOP challenger George Chambers, eking out a razor-thin victory (107,357 votes for Roush against 107,258 tallies for Chambers). After a recount, a newly elected Indiana governor Matthew Welsh issued a certificate of election to Roush in January 1961. The certificate was signed just after Welsh took office, and it had to be in the hands of the clerk of the U.S. House of Representatives the next day. A strike by airline pilots left many planes grounded, so a young Indianapolis lawyer, Andy Jacobs Jr., took on the assignment of hand delivering the certificate to the clerk in Washington, D.C., by nine o'clock in the morning. Jacobs left Indianapolis, drove all night, and arrived before the deadline. Congress certified Roush as the winner, and he was sworn in for a second term.

When Jacobs was elected to Congress from the Indianapolis area in 1964, one of the first individuals to assist the freshman lawmaker with orientation was Roush. Jacobs recalled that Roush helped him with office details and even showed him where to pick up his paycheck. He remembers Roush as "thoughtful and empathetic, a true gentleman," and noted that he once witnessed the congressman stopping to help a stranded driver change a tire along the busy Pennsylvania Turnpike, when many other motorists had passed him by.

In his early years in Congress, Roush's achievements centered on safeguarding Indiana's natural resources. He sponsored legislation to preserve the Indiana Dunes in northwestern Indiana, and he authored legislation creating three different reservoirs: Mississinewa, Salamonie, and Huntington. (Huntington Lake was renamed J. Edward Roush Lake in 1997.) The creation of these large reservoirs in north-central Indiana aided in efforts to control flooding and provided additional recreational space for the area. Roush was also a key proponent of the Rock Creek Watershed Bill passed in 1967, a landmark effort to promote soil conservation and to preserve rural land and control flooding.

Throughout the 1960s Roush supported most of the domestic legislation authored by presidents John Kennedy and Lyndon Johnson, establishing for himself a moderate reputation on national issues. The congressman is most noted for his early support on behalf of the school lunch program and federal aid to elementary and secondary education. He worked with Kennedy to fund the space program, and he became an early advocate for sending an American to the moon. The largely rural Fifth District backed Roush's work by reelecting him as its representative in races from 1962 to 1966.

Roush's political world, however, turned upside down in the 1968 congressional elections. Normally, state legislative and congressional redistricting occurs in the year following a census. The 1961 session of the Indiana General Assembly, though, failed in its reapportionment task, and the matter remained unresolved until 1967, when the state supreme court mandated redistricting. The Republican-controlled legislature redrew district maps to favor its candidates. Completed on February 14, 1968, the reapportionment was later dubbed the Saint Valentine Day's Massacre by Jacobs. Seeing his district given away in a deliberate move to gerrymander him into a less favorable political climate, Roush found himself now having to run in the new Fourth District if he wanted to remain in Congress past 1968. While he did not relish the upcoming difficult campaign, he accepted the opportunity to challenge incumbent E. Ross Adair for the seat.

Adair was an institution in Fort Wayne and northeastern Indiana. He was first elected in 1950 and had not had serious opposition for several elections. Like Roush, he had an outstanding war record. A ranking member of the House Armed Services Committee, Adair had won a reputation as a hard-working congressman backed by a district office with a good record of helping constituents. Adair and Roush were friends, and the GOP congressman had a strong rapport with other members of the Indiana delegation.

Roush considered his campaign to unseat Adair as the greatest political challenge of his career, and he knew it would be a monumental task to beat a man who had such a strong hold in northeastern Indiana. Roush also knew he was not known in the new district. The only holdover county in the Fourth was Huntington. Roush had to introduce himself to his new constituents in a hurry, and to win the election he would have to outwork and outsmart both Adair and one of he best Republican organizations in the country.

Matters in Washington did not help Roush's cause in this politically bitter year. Domestically, the country was being torn apart by the conflict over such issues as the civil rights movement, inflation, crime, the environment, and the Vietnam War. Even worse, the Democratic Party was in turmoil in both Washington and Indiana. President Johnson, a good friend of Roush, had been politically wounded by the country's problems and the challenge to his presidency by senators Robert Kennedy and Eugene McCarthy. Just a month before the Indiana primary, Johnson withdrew from the contest, further confusing the electorate. Indiana governor Roger Branigin ran as a Johnson stand-in against Kennedy and McCarthy in the May 7 Democratic presidential primary. The division in the Indiana Democratic Party caused by this three-way race became evident throughout the state. It became clear that every Democrat running for election had to struggle against a tidal wave of voter dissatisfaction with the Democratic Party.

As the fall campaign unfolded, a clear contrast between

Asked by an Indianapolis Star *reporter in 1984 if he might ever consider running for public office again, Roush noted: "I had my time. I served when it was appropriate and now it is time for others."*

the two candidates began to emerge. For Adair the solutions
were nonproblematic. Only an unpatriotic citizen would turn
his back on the boys in Vietnam at this stage of the fighting.
As tragic as the killings of Robert Kennedy and Martin
Luther King Jr. were, enacting legislation to restrict the flow
of firearms would only hurt the innocent individuals who
had a Second Amendment right under the U.S. Constitution
to purchase any gun of their choice. Civil rights for all was a
laudable goal, but this was not a matter in which the federal
government should be involved. Adair thought individual states
should address this issue, and they needed more time. As far
as the environment was concerned, he believed that enacting
more stringent water and air pollution controls would be
harmful to business and industry.

Taking similar stands might attract more support in
1968, but Roush sensed that times were changing and minds
were evolving. He believed that opposing the war, supporting
sensible gun control, voting for civil rights legislation, and
taking big business and agriculture interests to task for
polluting were the right stands to take, and perhaps vindication
might come from debating these issues. In every appearance
during the campaign, Roush sought to show the contrast
between himself and his opponent. He traveled the district
and called for an end to the war. Adair supported the stand
of Republican presidential candidate Richard Nixon and said
he would work with Nixon to bring an "honorable" end to
the conflict during the next administration. Roush espoused

strong support for the Civil Rights Act of 1968, which barred discrimination in the sale and rental of housing. Adair said Congress had not had time to study the legislation carefully and probably should not interfere in this area. Roush advocated legislation to prevent sewage, chemicals, and other waste from being dumped into lakes and rivers and advocated tighter restrictions on factories that polluted the air.

Roush had proved to be an energetic campaigner in his former district, and he campaigned with that same fervor in the new Fourth District. On evenings and weekends, legions of young people, including minorities, environmentalists, working people, and labor union members joined him as he walked the district in search of votes. Roush had the enthusiasm to coalesce around him a growing number of disenfranchised voters and potential supporters who believed his stands might change the country for the better. He became known as the Democratic Party's "walking apostle" as he went from town to town and county to county to discuss the issues and meet the voters. During one walk across the district, he completed 144 miles in eight days. A large shoe print emblazoned with his name became a familiar trademark of the campaign and was seen on brochures and bumper stickers.

On election day, November 5, 1968, approximately 215,000 residents cast their votes in the Fourth Congressional District. Roush ran ahead of the entire Democratic ticket, including Vice President Hubert Humphrey, Senator Birch Bayh, the state Democratic team, and all local candidates, but lost to Adair by approximately five thousand votes. This was a disastrous year for Indiana Democrats, with Bayh the lone statewide Democrat to win. On election night Roush took his defeat with humor and dignity. He termed the close race his "greatest campaign," and he thanked the legions of supporters who gathered at the old Keenan Hotel in downtown Fort Wayne.

It did not take Roush long to think about another run in the Fourth District in 1970. He was heartened by the encouragement he received as he went back to practice law, and he continued to speak around the area. By mid-1969 voter disenchantment was growing with the new president and Republicans in Congress regarding the issues Roush had raised in 1968. More people believed Roush was right when he spoke of ending the war, enacting environmental legislation to clean the air and water, and supporting civil rights for all Americans.

Roush decided to try again. In 1970 his campaign was better organized and better financed. He recruited more volunteers from all walks of life, and this time his name recognition matched Adair's. Roush was greeted and approached everywhere he went, and he walked and campaigned throughout the district with the same vigor he had done two yeas earlier. He participated in the first Earth Day in April 1970 and used the opportunity to cite the differences between the two candidates on environmental issues. The safe production of food and the elimination of hunger also became two of his main causes. Later in the campaign, Roush and

several volunteers from Huntington College participated in a
"walk for hunger" for twenty-five miles between Huntington
and Fort Wayne, collecting pledges and drawing attention to a
growing problem in America.

Despite a rumor that Adair, at age sixty-two, might retire
after twenty years in office, he decided to run, offering the
state the most exciting congressional race of the political
season. Anticipating a close contest, Adair and the GOP
brought in influential Republicans to offer support, including
Nixon, who visited the district in the fall. Numerous Adair
advertisements showed the president holding aloft Adair's arm
and admonishing voters: "I need this man in Washington."

Roush was more upbeat and confident as he walked in the
1970 campaign. The crowds were larger and more enthusiastic
than before, which helped generate positive media coverage
for his efforts. On election night, Roush upset the ten-term
incumbent, reversing the 5,000-vote deficit of 1968 to a 6,256-
vote plurality. Hundreds of euphoric Democrats gathered at the
old National Guard Armory on Clinton Street in downtown
Fort Wayne to celebrate Roush's triumph. Many of them were
the soldiers of the campaign trail who walked with him, and
others were the downtrodden who had been uplifted by his
campaign.

The Hoosier Democrat began his second tenure in
Congress in January 1971 and received a seat on the influential
Committee on Appropriations. With that post he had an
opportunity to advocate not only for programs in his district,

but also for national programs that he cared deeply about. In 1972 Roush cast a deciding vote in favor of providing more federal aid to education and for the continuation of the school lunch program. During the next six years in Congress he became a strong supporter for federal efforts to encourage merit promotions in the civil service. Roush also called for increased federal control of oil companies, setting a ceiling on federal spending, and ending the draft. On foreign policy, Roush voted for foreign-aid reductions, urged open relations with China, supported an $8 billion cut in defense spending, voiced support for curtailing nuclear proliferation, and called for a halt in Vietnam War bombing. For the Fourth District, the congressman acquired federal funds to build a new post office in downtown Fort Wayne, successfully sought funding for flood control projects, and garnered contracts for the local defense industry. Roush also worked on soil and water conservation efforts and urged preservation of Indiana's natural resources.

In 1972 Roush faced a tough challenge in Republican candidate Allan Bloom, a state senator. Early in the election it looked as thought it might be a good year for Democrats as Senator Edmund Muskie of Maine led Nixon in the polls, but in the fall, after South Dakota senator George McGovern won the nomination, many Democrats in Congress braced for tough elections. On November 2, 1972, Nixon swept forty-nine states and captured more than 60 percent of the popular vote, carrying Indiana by approximately 700,000 votes—one of his largest pluralities in any state. Nixon also won handily in the Fourth District by more than 65,000 votes. Roush survived the Republican landslide and won reelection by 5,835 votes. On election night he admitted it was a miracle he withstood the GOP's national dominance.

Two years later, Roush faced an equally formidable challenger in Walter Helmke, then a state senator from Fort Wayne. Despite the favorable attitude toward Democrats in this year of the Watergate scandal, the Fourth District remained a tough area to win. Helmke was from a well-known political family and was respected by Democrats as well as Republicans. Helmke recalled that as the GOP candidate he was considered more liberal than Roush by many voters because of his support in the Indiana Senate for the Equal Rights Amendment and for legislation to lower the voting age to eighteen. As chairman of the senate judiciary committee, Helmke also sponsored legislation to enact the *Rowe v. Wade* decision, legalizing abortion in the Hoosier State. In Congress Roush had supported a constitutional amendment outlawing abortion except to save the life of the mother. Helmke, who had been recruited to run by the Allen County Republican Party, agreed to make several joint appearances with Roush during the campaign. Roush again defeated his GOP challenger.

During the next two years Roush continued to work on issues that affected the nation and his district. He often stated that he worked hard for his constituents, but he felt he should always put the interests of his country first, even if that

put him at odds with the voters back home. This philosophy
began to haunt him as the 1976 campaign neared. America
was becoming more conservative, as the new political right
and the Christian Coalition emerged. For years Roush had
championed causes such as a national health insurance program
for catastrophic illnesses, enacting heavier fines for industries
that polluted lakes and rivers, elimination of tax advantages for
oil companies, block grants to states and localities for urban
renewal, increased federal aid for education and for funding
alternative forms of energy, and the creation of a national
institute for crime prevention in Washington, D.C. These
causes now earned him the charge of being too liberal for the
district and worse yet of being a big spender.

Helmke contemplated a rematch with Roush in 1976
but changed his mind because of an expanding legal business
and the death of his father. He was also certain that unseating
Roush would be next to impossible, despite the deepening
conservative mood of the district. Instead, he worked with
Orvas Beers, Allen County Republican chairman, to recruit
a candidate. Some believed that Roush, now fifty-six,
might retire after one more term. Polly Roush had stayed
in Huntington, and the congressman's commute home
each weekend was beginning to wear on him. Beers, on the
advice of Ernie Williams, a *Fort Wayne News-Sentinel* editor,
persuaded a twenty-nine-year-old newspaper executive, also
from Huntington, to run. His name: Dan Quayle. Adair,
Bloom, and Helmke had all hailed from Allen County, and

GOP officials believed that a candidate from outside the Fort Wayne area might have a better chance at carrying some of the outlying counties in the Fourth District.

At first Quayle seemed reluctant to challenge Roush, contemplating instead a run for the state legislature. Quayle's father, James, who was the publisher of several daily newspapers, including the *Huntington Herald-Press*, told him he could not win a race against such a well-entrenched incumbent. "All the big guns in the district had tried to beat him [Roush] and failed—two well-known state senators for example," Dan Quayle remembered. "Nobody was anxious to run against him." Helmke believed Quayle was ultimately persuaded that he could run a close race in 1976 and perhaps be the front-runner in 1978, particularly if Roush retired.

During the campaign, Roush emphasized his strong constituent service record and some of his more conservative votes such as cutting foreign aid, supporting a pro-life amendment, and putting a ceiling on federal spending. He also appealed to populists through his work to require more disclosure from lobbyists, for voting against a congressional pay hike, and for working to enact the 911 emergency telephone system nationwide.

Bruce Stier, a Fort Wayne attorney, served as youth volunteer coordinator for the Roush campaign that year. He had been a volunteer for the congressman's previous campaigns in the Fourth District. Although Stier had no trouble recruiting young people to participate in walks, stuff envelopes, and work

phone banks, he sensed the Roush organization was not quite
as strong as in previous years. To strengthen the campaign,
Stier organized a neighborhood block captain system in key
precincts, sensing that Roush was going to need more help than
usual in traditionally Democratic areas of Fort Wayne.

Quayle ran an aggressive and visible campaign and labeled
himself the true conservative of the two candidates. Citing

*Dan Quayle received congratulations from Roush on election night
in 1976 after defeating the longtime incumbent congressman. One
astonished Fort Wayne political reporter commented: "Quayle came out
of nowhere to run against Ed Roush. No one knew who he [Quayle] was.
I had been around politicians in Fort Wayne for years; and I had never
heard of him."*

Roush's many votes in support of nationalized health care and for federal aid to education and job training, Quayle charged that the congressman was out of touch with Fourth District voters.

Quayle upset Roush by approximately 19,000 votes on election day, a stunning win. "Roush didn't take me seriously until the last ten days," said Quayle. "And then it was too late." Although disappointed with the outcome, Roush held his head high and made an unprecedented move by walking over to the Republican celebration and personally congratulating the new congressman-elect. The next day Roush was back at his office in the federal building in downtown Fort Wayne. Quayle was soon on his way to the national stage, and Roush was content to return to Huntington to travel, relax, and spend more time with Polly and their growing family.

Roush left office in January 1977 and returned to the practice of law. Until his death on March 26, 2004, Roush worked on numerous committees, espoused various charitable causes, spoke out on issues, helped Democratic candidates from around the state, and served for six months as interim president of Huntington College. During his political career, Roush played more than just a passing role in the education of a people and the governing of a nation. He worked at the forefront of issues to improve education, health care, and job training. Perhaps his greatest legacy was his sponsorship of numerous pieces of legislation to preserve natural resources, fight pollution, fund flood control projects, and enact the 911 emergency telephone system across the United States. His passion to serve the country in so many ways inspired many in subsequent generations to enter public service.

FOR FURTHER READING Fenno, Richard F. *The Making of a Senator: Dan Quayle*. Washington, D.C.: CQ Press, 1989. | O'Callaghan, Phyllis. "Ed Roush, Father of 911." *Indiana Alumni Magazine* 64 (January/February 2002): 40–43. | Walsh, Justin E. *The Centennial History of the Indiana General Assembly, 1816–1978*. Indianapolis: Select Committee on the Centennial History of the Indiana General Assembly, 1987.

8

William Ruckelshaus

One of the greatest dramas in American political history played out more than thirty years ago in Washington, D.C. The Watergate scandal snared President Richard Nixon and propelled a Hoosier political leader into the national spotlight. It was the unexpected role of Bill Ruckelshaus in that investigation that ultimately led to the beginning of the end of Nixon's presidency. Ruckelshaus's action showed courage in the face of a president and an administration that had strayed from the course of governing a nation to a course of lying and cover-up. The decision of Ruckelshaus in the so-called Saturday Night Massacre of October 20, 1973, reminded Hoosier citizens that honesty and integrity still mattered in the minds of their leaders.

In the fall of 1973 Ruckelshaus served in the fourth and perhaps the most important position he had assumed since Nixon took office on January 20, 1969. Ruckelshaus was Deputy Attorney General of the United States, serving under

Attorney General Elliot Richardson. Prior to this position, Ruckelshaus had briefly worked as acting director of the Federal Bureau of Investigation in early 1973. He was the first director of the Environmental Protection Agency from 1970 to 1973, and he started out in the Nixon administration as an Assistant Attorney General in the Civil Division in 1969 and 1970. Prior to coming to Washington, Ruckelshaus served one term in the Indiana House of Representatives and was majority leader of the Republican caucus. In the early 1960s he was a chief counsel in the Indiana Attorney General's office and attorney for the minority senate Republicans in the general assembly. He attracted national attention, and the attention of Nixon, when he came within sixty-five thousand votes of unseating incumbent Democratic U.S. senator Birch Bayh in 1968. It was one of the most exciting and closest Senate races in the country, and it helped to propel Ruckelshaus to Washington and into the Nixon administration in January 1969.

William Doyle Ruckelshaus was born on July 24, 1932, in Indianapolis. His parents were John and Marion Doyle Ruckelshaus. His father and grandfather were prominent Republicans in Marion County, where his grandfather had served as prosecuting attorney and as chairman of the Indiana Republican Party. His father, John, was active nationally in the Republican Party and served on its platform committee from 1920 to 1960, attended many GOP national conventions, and considered running for the U.S. Senate from Indiana in 1944.

Ruckelshaus graduated from Princeton University in 1957

INDIANAPOLIS STAR

In looking back at the number of positions he occupied in government, William Ruckelshaus observed that he "had an awful lot of jobs in my lifetime, and in moving from one to another, have had the opportunity to think about what makes them worthwhile. I've concluded there are four important criteria: interest, excitement, challenge, and fulfillment. I've never worked anywhere where I could find all four to quite the same extent as at EPA [Environmental Protection Agency]."

after serving in the army. He received his law degree from Harvard University in 1960 and then joined his family's law firm of Ruckelshaus, Bobbitt, and O'Connor in Indianapolis. On May 12, 1962, he married Jill Elizabeth Strickland; the couple had five children. Ruckelshaus practiced law in the early 1960s while also serving as Deputy Attorney General for Indiana from 1961 to 1965 under Attorney General Ed Steer. Walter Helmke, a former state senator, was prosecuting attorney from Allen County at that time. He often worked with Ruckelshaus, who argued all homicide case convictions before the Indiana Supreme Court. "You could always count on him to back the murder convictions of local prosecutors, and he developed a strong reputation among us," noted Helmke.

From 1965 to 1967 Ruckelshaus was the attorney for the state senate Republican caucus, which was in the minority after the 1964 election. That year he was also an unsuccessful candidate for the U.S. House of Representatives in the Republican primary. Running as a moderate, he was soundly defeated by a more conservative Barry Goldwater Republican, who went down to defeat in November. After losing in May 1964, Ruckelshaus set his sights on a seat in the Indiana House of Representatives in the 1966 election. He easily won the election and became one of sixty-six Republicans in the hundred-member house. Partly because of his impressive victory and partly because he had great knowledge of the legislative system, Ruckelshaus became majority leader of the Republican caucus in his first year as a state representative.

He became the first freshman state representative ever to serve as majority leader, and he was voted the most outstanding Republican legislator of 1967 by statewide political reporters. Bill Latz, a former state representative from Fort Wayne, remembers his colleague, who appointed him to the Constitution Review Committee, was viewed as a future House Speaker in the mold of the much revered Otis Bowen, who served as governor from 1973 to 1981.

Ruckelshaus was only thirty-five and in his second year of his first and only term in the general assembly when he was approached to run for the U.S. Senate in 1968. Birch Bayh had won the seat in an unexpected upset over Homer Capehart in 1962 by less than eleven thousand votes. In a year that was looking to be favorable to the Republicans nationally and in Indiana, Bayh appeared to be vulnerable. Ray Rizzo worked in the state legislative council when Ruckelshaus served in the general assembly. He remembered the one-term legislator as "very honest, personable and sincere, a real people person."

During the Senate campaign, Ruckelshaus sometimes answered questions unrelated to a national campaign. At one press conference a reporter asked about a state proposal promoting pari-mutuel betting. Rizzo noted that most candidates would have refused to answer a question not related to their own campaign, but Ruckelshaus spoke in favor of the proposal, which may have cost him votes with conservative Republicans in Indiana. Yet, he ran an aggressive and well-funded campaign for the Senate and came close to winning,

*As head of the EPA, Ruckelshaus (far right) joins Wyoming Democratic
Senator Gale McGee (left), chairman of the Senate Appropriations
Committee, and Nathaniel Reed (center), Assistant Secretary of the
Interior, during a 1971 Senate inquest into the death of fifty bald and
golden eagles.*

as Nixon swept the state by more than a quarter-million votes and Republicans won every other statewide office, picking up congressional seats and continuing a firm lock on the Indiana General Assembly.

While he lost an opportunity to represent his state in the Senate, Ruckelshaus gained an opportunity to serve his state and the nation in the Nixon administration. He was one of a number of defeated Republican candidates to be brought into the Justice Department by Attorney General John Mitchell. Ruckelshaus was appointed Assistant Attorney General in the Civil Division in January 1969. One of his early responsibilities was to tour college campuses across the nation to hear concerns and to improve communication with students.

When Nixon established the Environmental Protection Agency in 1970, he appointed Ruckelshaus as its first director. Ruckelshaus immediately worked to enforce the regulatory powers that were assigned to him through the Clean Air and Water acts and warned cities to stop the flow of raw sewage into the nation's waterways. In 1971 Ruckelshaus cited large corporations for dumping chemicals and other waste into rivers and lakes. He also ordered other large companies to reduce the sulphur dioxide being emitted and to reduce ash emissions, and he influenced the automobile industry to make cleaner engines. In his three years at EPA, Ruckelshaus's work received the approval of conservationists for his enforcement of clean air and water standards and for proposing an alternate route for the Alaskan pipeline.

As the Watergate scandal unfolded in 1972 and 1973, various government officials became casualties of the administration's deceit and cover-up. As the complex story unraveled, public opinion polls showed that the president's credibility fell so low that his ability to govern the nation came into question. Many of Nixon's top aides and former cabinet members were implicated in either the scandal or the cover-up of the June 17, 1972, break-in of the Democratic National Committee offices in Washington. One of the fist resignations was that of L. Patrick Gray, acting director of the Federal Bureau of Investigation. On April 30, 1973, Nixon appointed Ruckelshaus to become the second acting director of the FBI in less than a year. Ruckelshaus, however, stayed only a short time at the FBI. In May former attorney general Mitchell and former commerce secretary Maurice Stans were indicted for their involvement in the Watergate scandal. Shortly before that, Attorney General Richard Kleindienst had resigned his post as well.

Nixon needed a new team in the Justice Department to restore lost credibility. He quickly appointed Secretary of Defense Elliot Richardson to be attorney general and gave him the authority to appoint a special prosecutor to conduct an independent investigation of Watergate. Richardson appointed Archibald Cox, a Harvard law school professor and former U.S. Solicitor General. The president said Cox would have "absolute authority to make all decisions bearing upon the prosecution of the Watergate case and related matters." He promised Cox "total cooperation."

Ruckelshaus was only forty-one when he was appointed to his fourth major position in the Nixon administration in four years. He was transferred over to the Justice Department from the FBI to become deputy attorney general under Richardson. According to Stanley Kutler, author of *The Wars of Watergate*, the new deputy had a "well earned reputation as a moderate man." The president regarded Ruckelshaus as a "Mr. Clean" and someone not only bright but also well respected. For his part, Ruckelshaus had served Nixon in several capacities but began to lose faith in the president while acting director of the FBI in the spring of 1973. Ruckelshaus saw the FBI as "torn asunder but not falling apart" due to the Watergate scandal. He had visited with the president in late April 1973 and asked him if he had been involved in the scandal. Nixon gave him "a very convincing argument that he would not be implemented in any wrongdoing." However, he warned the president that he would have to be more specific in his denials of any role in the cover-up or his critics would never be satisfied.

As Kutler noted, Ruckelshaus saw the Watergate break in as "trivial but what happened afterwards was not trivial, it was profound." In a commencement address to students at Ohio State University, Ruckelshaus recognized the declining credibility of the federal government due to the scandal. "To our great country's misfortune," he noted, "the Watergate has accelerated that process." Ruckelshaus emphasized the necessity for maintaining faith that government could and would bring lawmakers to account. He directly confronted those who wished to dismiss the affair as "politics as usual." To do so, he warned only invited "cynical abuse" of the political process. Quoting Ralph Waldo Emerson, he concluded: "This time 'like all times is a very good one, if we but know what to do with it.'"

As Cox began his duties as special prosecutor, a Senate select committee also began hearings on the matter in the summer of 1973. In August it was revealed the president had initiated a number of tape recordings of conversations with top aides regarding Watergate. The Senate committee and Cox demanded that Nixon turn over specific records of his talks with John Dean, John Mitchell, H. R. Haldeman, and John Ehrlichman. The president refused, citing executive privilege and indicating he wanted to protect communications within his office. Cox issued a subpoena demanding that nine tapes be given to a grand jury. Judge John Sirica ruled in favor of the subpoena, and his ruling was upheld by an appellate court on October 12. Ruckelshaus recalled years later that Nixon was quite concerned about the consequences of releasing the tapes and wanted desperately to keep them from the public.

Not wanting to surrender the tapes to the special prosecutor, Nixon sought to arrange for a third party, Mississippi senator John Stennis, a former judge, to listen to a summary of the subpoenaed tapes prepared by the White House. The president also demanded that Cox not submit any future subpoenas for tapes or other documents relating to the Watergate issue.

Needless to say, Cox refused to accept the arrangement from the White House. This action set up the most dramatic moment of the Watergate scandal, which became known as the "Saturday Night Massacre." Incensed that Cox would refuse his offer, Nixon ordered his dismissal from the position for which the administration had pledged total cooperation just months before.

Ruckelshaus said Cox sought to "thoroughly and dispassionately look into the allegations of wrongdoing directed at many White House employees, including the man who had asked me to be the Director of the FBI and later Deputy Attorney General. Cox and I communicated almost daily over a period of several weeks. Our relationship could not have been better. I think is it fair to say we were both determined to carry out our assignments as well as possible." Gary Baise, an assistant to Ruckelshaus and later a deputy attorney general himself, said his boss would only consider firing the special prosecutor for "extraordinary improprieties, something that had not occurred" on the part of Cox.

In addition to the simmering Watergate investigation, another story was breaking in Washington. During the summer of 1973, Vice President Spiro Agnew was being investigated on charges of accepting illegal payments in return for favors during his public career as county executive in Baltimore, governor of Maryland, and even as vice president. On October 10, Agnew filed a nolo contendre plea to the charges and resigned his office. Within days, Nixon nominated House Minority

Ruckelshaus leaves the Justice Department in Washington, D.C., on October 20, 1973, shortly before President Richard Nixon announced he had accepted Attorney General Elliot Richardson's resignation and fired Special Prosecutor Archibald Cox.

Leader Gerald Ford of Michigan to become vice president.
As deputy attorney general, it was the job of Ruckelshaus to
travel to Grand Rapids to conduct a routine field investigation
of Ford and interview everyone who had dealings with
the congressman. Before leaving on Monday, October 15,
Richardson warned his deputy that Nixon was preparing to
fire Cox. Surprised, Ruckelshaus responded, "don't worry, he'll
never do it. The American people won't tolerate it."

On Wednesday, October 17, Ruckelshaus returned early to
Washington from Grand Rapids on a request from Richardson.
Nixon had advised the Justice Department to warn Cox not
to pursue additional tapes other than the summaries given
to Stennis. Cox refused the order on Friday, October 19. On
Saturday, October 20, Nixon ordered Richardson to fire Cox,
through his chief of staff, Alexander Haig. Richardson refused
and met with the president at the White House that afternoon
to offer his resignation. Nixon asked him to carry out the order
and delay his resignation until an unfolding crisis in the Middle
East was stabilized. Richardson replied: "I can only say that I
believe my resignation is in the public interest."

Haig next went to Ruckelshaus. In his book on Watergate,
author Fred Emery said the deputy attorney general noted
that he was bound by the oath he had taken and by the
pledges he had made to the U.S. Senate to support Cox.
"Your commander in chief has given you an order," Haig said.
"You have no alternative." Ruckelshaus responded, "Except
to resign." (He had already written a letter of resignation

before his meeting with Haig.) He also told Haig that Cox had done nothing to warrant his removal as special prosecutor and that he would have to go to the third in command at the Justice Department, Solicitor General Robert Bork, to get the job done. According to Emery, Nixon's memoirs noted that Ruckelshaus resigned, but the White House stated that night he had been "discharged." Haig later disclosed that Nixon had said of Ruckelshaus, "We don't owe him anything but a good kick in the ass. Ruckelshaus only wants to return to Indiana to run for the Senate."

Ruckelshaus remembered that Bork was angry about being forced into the position of firing Cox. Bork told him he would carry out the order but he too would later resign his position. He felt refusal to carry out the order might bring more instability to the Justice Department. He met later in the day with Nixon and the president told him he wanted "a prosecution not a persecution." Bork later dismissed Cox. The FBI sealed off the offices of Richardson, Ruckelshaus, and Cox "at the request of the White House." According to the *Washington Post*, the FBI was ordered to be sure nothing was taken out of the three men's offices.

Ruckelshaus later recalled, "I do not believe the decision to resign was a difficult one. When you accept a presidential appointment you must remind yourself there are lines over which you will not step. The line for me was considerably behind where I would have been standing had I fired Cox. In this case, the line was bright and the decision was simple."

The public reaction to the Saturday Night Massacre could not have been worse for the Nixon administration. Thousands of Americans sent Congress and the president letters and telegrams protesting the firings of three worthy public servants. Many believe this was the beginning of the end of the Nixon administration, as the president appeared to be placing himself above the law. The action by the White House cost Nixon support among the American people and with key Republican members of the Senate. There soon began serious discussion of impeachment in the halls of Congress.

Newsweek magazine praised Cox, Richardson, and Ruckelshaus as "Three men of high principle." Others in the media denounced the administration for this "reckless act" and for using "Gestapo tactics." The White House miscalculated how the public would react. Chesterfield Smith, president of the American Bar Association, said the actions threatened "the rule of law and the administration of justice." He praised "three great lawyers—Richardson, Ruckelshaus, and Cox—who honor and cherish the tradition of the legal profession and who place ethics and professional honor before public office." Even supporters of the president urged a separate investigation to see how the White House could cause such a manipulation in the Justice Department. Latz recalled that Ruckelshaus "thumbed his nose at all the greed in politics because of his fine character. Because of him, the government remained stable, and the Constitution was upheld."

Late in the day of Saturday, October 20, 1973,

Ruckelshaus ended his five years with the Nixon administration without calling a news conference or uttering disparaging remarks about the president he had long served. His role in the controversy had made him a national celebrity, but it had hurt him among some Hoosier Republican voters, who believed he had been disloyal to the president. For the next few years, Ruckleshaus served as an attorney with the firm of Ruckelshaus, Beveridge, Fairbanks, and Diamond. Efforts were made to persuade him to return to Indiana to again run for the U.S. Senate, but Ruckelshaus refused. "I wanted to get rid of some of the emotion of being in public life," he said. "While I wanted to be a United States Senator, I just could not pass the acid test of politics of that era. It took me about nine months of concentrated effort to stabilize my family and personal existence. But it happened, and in general, my life has been made far richer as a result of my service in government."

While saying "one year of Watergate is enough," Nixon hoped a new special prosecutor and a new year would change the way Americans looked at the scandal. The president, however, became further mired in the controversy throughout 1974. The House of Representatives began impeachment hearings in the spring. Evidence was presented that Nixon was involved in the cover-up of the burglary of the Democratic National Committee as early as June 23, 1972, less than a week after the incident. With support from his own party quickly disintegrating, Nixon resigned the presidency on August 9.

In 1975 Ruckelshaus relocated with his family to Seattle,

Washington, where he served as a senior vice president of the Weyerhaeuser Company. According to Rizzo, Ruckelshaus was on Ford's shortlist as a vice presidential running mate in 1976, and Governor Otis Bowen was prepared to give the nominating speech at the Republican National Convention. Baise said Texas Senator John Tower came out adamantly opposed to the vice presidential nod because of a stand Ruckelshaus made as EPA director about a pesticide used in Texas. Baise thought his boss's reputation would have "inoculated Ford from criticism for pardoning Nixon" in 1974. However, Ford chose Senator Robert Dole of Kansas. The Ford-Dole ticket lost to former Governor Jimmy Carter of Georgia.

In 1983 Ruckelshaus returned to Washington to serve again as director of the EPA under President Ronald Reagan following the resignation of Ann Gorsuch Burford. Reagan needed a leader with integrity to improve the staff and boost morale in the agency. Ruckelshaus improved working conditions at the EPA and also oversaw the removal of the pesticide ethylene dibromide from U.S. agricultural use. He also reaffirmed EPA's commitment to a federal-state partnership to restore and protect the Chesapeake Bay, and he helped the federal agency institute tighter controls on hazardous waste management.

After completing his second term at the EPA in 1985, Ruckelshaus returned to Seattle and joined the law firm of Perkins Coie. He served as chief executive officer of Browning-Ferris Industries Inc. from 1988 to 1999. He currently serves as a principal in the Madrona Investment Group, a private investment firm in Seattle. In late 1988, Indiana governor Bob Orr offered the Senate seat being vacated by Vice President-Elect Dan Quayle to Ruckelshaus. "I refused the appointment partly because I did not have a residence in Indiana and partly because of my business and family responsibilities in Washington State," Ruckelshaus said. Orr appointed Dan Coats to the Senate seat.

The Watergate scandal was a deep scar on the history of the presidency. The deceit in the Nixon White House claimed many careers. Some were seen, however, as rising above the fray of the scandal and standing up for principal instead of trying to protect a corrupt administration. Ruckelshaus was one of the individuals who stood up and gained a place in Indiana history, becoming one of the few bright stars in an otherwise sea of corruption during the two years of Watergate. He continues to serve today in many capacities in both the private and public sectors with honesty and integrity. "Bill is a giant. He is the real deal," said Rizzo.

For Further Reading Bernstein, Carl, and Bob Woodward. *All the President's Men*. New York: Simon and Schuster, 1974. | Emery, Fred. *Watergate: The Corruption of American Politics and the Fall of Richard Nixon*. New York: Touchstone, 1994. | Kutler, Stanley. *The Wars of Watergate: The Last Crisis of Richard Nixon*. New York: Knopf, 1990.

Index